THE
FBI

KNOW YOUR GOVERNMENT

THE
FBI

ST. GABRIEL SCHOOL

Fred L. Israel
Professor of American History
City College of New York

INTRODUCTORY ESSAY BY
Arthur M. Schlesinger, jr.
Albert Schweitzer Professor of the Humanities
City University of New York

353.5
ISR

CHELSEA HOUSE PUBLISHERS
NEW YORK   NEW HAVEN   PHILADELPHIA

Project Editor: John Selfridge
Associate Editors: Paula Edelson, Linda Grossman, Perry Scott King
Editorial Coordinator: Karyn Gullen Browne
Art Director: Susan Lusk
Layout: Irene Friedman
Cover and Design: Deborah Daly
Picture Research: Susan Quist, Elizabeth Terhune

3 5 7 9 8 6 4 2

Library of Congress Cataloging in Publication Data
Israel, Fred L.
    The FBI.

    (Know your government)
    Bibliography: p.
    Includes index.
    Summary: A history of the Federal Bureau of
Investigation from its founding to the present
describing its functions, procedures, crime-detecting
techniques, and its influence on American society.
    1. United States. Federal Bureau of Investigation—
Juvenile literature. [1. United States. Federal Bureau
of Investigation] I. Title. II. Series: Know your
government (New York, N.Y.)
HV8141.I83   1985   353.0074   85-21292

ISBN 0-87754-821-8

Photos courtesy of AP/Wide World Photos, UPI, The Bettmann Archive, and the
Federal Bureau of Investigation

CONTENTS

cop. 1

Fred L. Israel is Professor of American History at the City College of New York. He is the author of *Nevada's Key Pittman* and has co-edited *A History of American Presidential Elections* and *The Justices of the United States Supreme Court.* His book, *Franklin Delano Roosevelt,* is part of the Chelsea House World Leaders series for young adults.

Arthur M. Schlesinger, jr., served in the White House as special assistant to Presidents Kennedy and Johnson. He is the acclaimed author of numerous works in American history and has twice been awarded the Pulitzer Prize. He taught history at Harvard for many years and is currently Albert Schweitzer Professor of the Humanities at the City College of New York.

Government:
Crises of Confidence

Arthur M. Schlesinger, jr.

From the start, Americans have regarded their government with a mixture of reliance and mistrust. The men who founded the republic did not doubt the indispensability of government. "If men were angels," observed the 51st Federalist Paper, "no government would be necessary." But men are not angels. Since human beings are subject to wicked as well as to noble impulses, government was deemed essential to assure freedom and order. "Government, like dress," Thomas Paine wrote in the year of the Declaration of Independence, "is the badge of lost innocence . . . rendered necessary by the inability of moral virtue to govern the world."

At the same time, the American revolutionaries, as they had made clear in the Declaration of Independence, knew that government could also become a source of injury and oppression. The men who gathered in Philadelphia in the summer of 1787 to give the new republic its constitution therefore had two purposes in mind. They wanted to establish a strong central authority, and they wanted equally to limit that central authority's capacity to abuse its power. "You must first enable the government to control the governed," the 51st Federalist declared; "and in the next place oblige it to control itself."

In order to prevent the abuse of power, the Founding Fathers wrote two basic principles into the new Constitution. The principle of federalism divided power between the state governments and the central authority. The principle of the separation of powers subdivided the central authority itself into three independent and coordinate branches—the executive, the legislative and the judiciary—so that, in the words of the Federalist, "each may be a check on the other." Government in its largest sense embraces state and local as well as national government, and it embraces all three branches of the national government. But, as Alexander Hamilton noted in the 72nd Federalist, government "in its most usual, and perhaps its most precise signification . . . falls peculiarly within the province of the executive department." When Americans speak of "the government," we generally mean the executive arm of the national government. It is in this sense that the *Know Your Government* series presents the history of the major executive departments and agencies.

The Constitution did not plan the executive branch in any detail. Article II, after vesting the executive power in the President, assumed the existence of "executive Departments" without specifying what these departments should be. This left the first President and Congress considerable latitude in organizing the executive arm. Congress began in 1789 by creating the Departments of State, Treasury, and War. The secretaries in charge of these departments made up President Washington's first cabinet. Congress also provided the President a legal officer, and President Washington soon invited the Attorney General, as he was called, to attend cabinet meetings. But the Attorney General remained a part-time job until 1853, and his department, the Department of Justice, was not established until 1870. As need required, Congress created more executive departments: Navy (1798); Postmaster General (raised to cabinet status in 1829); Interior (1849); Agriculture (raised to cabinet status in 1889); Commerce and Labor (1903, divided

7

into separate departments in 1913); Health, Education and Welfare (1953, divided in 1980 into departments of Health and Human Services and of Education); Housing and Urban Development (1966); Transportation (1966); Energy (1977).

The word cabinet does not appear in the Constitution; and in its American form the cabinet has never implied the collective decisions and responsibility that define the cabinet in Great Britain and other parliamentary democracies. In Britain, as John Adams, the second President noted, the cabinet ministers are everything; in the United States, "the ministers are responsible for nothing, the President for everything." George Washington, while he conscientiously consulted his secretaries, reserved the basic decisions for himself. Andrew Jackson flatly declined to submit questions to a cabinet vote. "I have accustomed myself to receive with respect the opinion of others," he said, "but always take the responsibility of deciding for myself." Abraham Lincoln, according to the old story, did once submit a question to vote, disagreed with his cabinet and ruled: "Ayes one, noes seven. The ayes have it."

Setting up the cabinet was only the first step in organizing the American state. With almost no guidance from the Constitution, President Washington, ably seconded by Alexander Hamilton, his brilliant Secretary of the Treasury, did an extraordinary job in equipping the infant republic with a working administrative structure. The Federalists believed both in executive energy and executive accountability and set high standards for public appointments. The system they devised established its moral authority in a surprisingly short time. The Jeffersonian opposition had less faith than the Hamiltonians in strong government and preferred local government to the central authority. But when Jefferson himself became President in 1801, though he set out to change the direction of policy, he found no reason to alter the framework the Federalists had erected.

By 1801 there were about 3000 federal civilian employees in a nation of a little more than 5 million people. Growth in territory and population steadily enlarged national responsibilities. Thirty years later, when Jackson was President, there were over 11,000 government workers in a nation of 13 million. The federal establishment was increasing at a faster rate than the population.

Jackson's Presidency brought about significant changes in the federal service. He believed that the executive branch contained too many officials who saw their jobs "as a species of property" and as "a means of promoting individual interest." Against the idea of a permanent service based on life tenure, Jackson argued for the periodic redistribution of federal offices, contending that this was the democratic way and that official duties could be made "so plain and simple that men of intelligence may readily qualify themselves for their performance." He called this policy rotation-in-office. His opponents, rejoicing in the remark by a Jacksonian politician that "to the victor belong the spoils of the enemy," called it the spoils system.

In fact, partisan legend exaggerated the extent of Jackson's removals. More than eighty percent of federal officeholders retained their jobs. Jackson discharged no larger a proportion of government workers than Jefferson had done a generation earlier. But the rise in these years of mass political parties gave federal patronage new importance as a means of building the party and of rewarding activists. Jackson's successors were less restrained in the distribution of spoils. As the federal establishment grew — nearly 40,000 by 1861 — the politicization of the public service excited increasing concern.

After the Civil War the spoils system became a major political issue. Highminded men condemned it as the root of all political evil. The spoilsmen, said the

8

British commentator James Bryce, "have distorted and depraved the mechanism of politics." Patronage, by giving jobs to unqualified, incompetent and dishonest persons, lowered the standards of public service, and nourished corrupt political machines. Office-seekers pursued Presidents and cabinet secretaries without mercy. "Patronage," said Ulysses S. Grant after his Presidency, "is the bane of the Presidential office." "Every time I appoint someone to office," said another political leader, "I make a hundred enemies and one ingrate."

George William Curtis, the president of the National Civil Service Reform League, summed up the indictment. He said,

> the theory which perverts public trusts into party spoils, making public employment dependent upon personal favor and not on proved merit, necessarily ruins the self-respect of public employes, destroys the function of party in a republic, prostitutes elections into a desperate strife for personal profit, and degrades the national character by lowering the moral tone and standard of the country.

The object of civil service reform was to promote efficiency and honesty in the public service and to bring about the ethical regeneration of public life. Over bitter opposition from politicians, the reformers in 1883 passed the Pendleton Act, establishing a bipartisan Civil Service Commission, competitive examinations, and appointment on merit. The Pendleton Act also gave the President authority to extend by executive order the number of "classified" jobs — that is, jobs subject to the merit system. The act applied initially only to about 14,000 of the more than 100,000 federal positions. But by the end of the 19th century 40 percent of federal jobs had moved into the classified category. The United States at last had the basis for a neutral, non-partisan, expert federal service.

Civil service reform was in part a response to the growing complexity of American life. As society grew more organized and problems more technical, official duties were no longer so plain and simple that any person of intelligence could perform them. In public service, as in other areas, the all-round man was yielding ground to the specialist, the amateur to the professional. "Nonprofessionalism is nonefficiency," Professor Woodrow Wilson wrote in 1901. America, he said, must develop "expert organization, if our government [is] to be preserved." The excesses of the spoils system thus provoked the counter-ideal of scientific public administration, separate from politics and, as far as possible, insulated against it.

The cult of the expert, however, had its own excesses. The idea that administration could be divorced from policy was an illusion. And, in the realm of policy, the expert, however much segregated from partisan politics, can never attain perfect objectivity. He remains the prisoner of his own set of values. It is these values rather than technical expertise that determine fundamental judgments of public policy. To turn over such judgments to experts, moreover, would be to abandon democracy itself; for in a democracy final decisions must be made by the people and their elected representatives. "The business of the expert," the British political scientist Harold Laski rightly said, "is to be on tap and not on top."

Politics in any event were too deeply ingrained in American folkways for the civil service to gain the same power and immunity that civil servants enjoyed in France or Great Britain. This did not mean that there was not intermittent tension within the executive branch between the presidential government, elected every four years by the people, and the permanent government, which saw Presidents come and go while it went on forever. Presidents tended to explain resistance by the permanent government in terms of political disagreement with administration policies. More often this resistance was politically neutral and sprang rather from the bureaucratic commitment to doing things as they had been done before. Sometimes the permanent government in its conservatism knew better than its political masters; sometimes it opposed or sabotaged valuable new initiatives. In the end a strong President with effective cabinet secretaries could make the permanent government responsive to presidential purpose, but it was often an exasperating struggle.

The struggle within the executive branch was less important, however, than the growing impatience with bureaucracy in society as a whole. The 20th century saw a considerable expansion of the federal establishment. The Great Depression and the New Deal led the national government to take on a variety of new economic and social responsibilities. In addition to the executive departments, the New Deal set up its famous alphabetical agencies and extended the federal regulatory apparatus. By 1940, in a nation now of 130 million people, the number of federal workers for the first time passed the one million mark. The Second World War brought federal civilian employment to 3.8 million in 1945. With peace, the federal establishment declined to around 2 million by 1950. Then growth resumed, reaching 2.8 million by the 1980s.

The New Deal years saw rising criticism of 'big government' and 'bureaucracy.' Businessmen resented federal regulation, whether with regard to minimum wages, maximum hours, unfair trade and labor practices, holding companies, or the stock exchange. Conservatives worried about the impact of paternalistic government on individual self-reliance, on community responsibility and on economic and personal freedom. The inevitable result of bureaucratic rule, said Herbert Hoover, was "this host of government agents spread out over the land, limiting men's honest activities, conferring largesse and benefits, directing, interfering, disseminating propaganda, spying on, threatening the people and prosecuting for a new host of crimes."

The nation in effect renewed the old debate between Hamilton and Jefferson in the early republic, though with an ironic exchange of positions. For the Hamiltonian constituency, the "rich and well-born," once the advocate of affirmative government, now condemned government intervention, while the Jeffersonian constituency, the plain people, once the advocate of a weak central government and of states' rights, now favored government intervention. This exchange of positions indeed had begun long before. It once reminded Abraham Lincoln of two drunks who engaged in a fight with their overcoats on and "ended in each having fought himself *out* of his own coat and *into* that of the other. If the two leading parties of this day are really identical with the two in the days of Jefferson and Adams, they have performed the same feat as the two drunken men."

In the 1980s, with the Presidency of Ronald Reagan, the debate has burst out with unusual intensity. Government intervention, the conservative indictment runs, abridges liberty and stifles enterprise. It is inefficient, wasteful, and arbitrary. It disturbs the harmony of the self-adjusting market and creates worse troubles than those it purports to solve. "Government is not the solution to the problem," Reagan said in his first inaugural address. "Government is the problem." Get government off our backs, according to the popular cliche, and our problems will solve themselves. When government is necessary, let it be at the local level, as close as possible to the people. Above all, stop the inexorable growth of the federal government.

In fact, for all the talk about the 'swollen' and 'bloated' bureaucracy, the federal establishment has not been growing as inexorably as many Americans seem to believe. In 1949, it consisted of 2.1 million people. Thirty years later, while the

10

country had grown by 70 million, the federal force had grown only by 750,000. Federal workers are a smaller percentage of the population in 1985 than they were in 1955—or in 1940. The federal establishment, in short, has not kept pace with population growth. Moreover, more than a third of the federal civilian work force—over a million—are in national defense, and another 660,000 deliver the mail. Together defense and the postal service account for 60 percent of federal employment.

Why then the widespread idea about the remorseless growth of government? It is partly because in the 1960s the national government assumed new and intrusive functions: affirmative action in civil rights; environmental protection; safety and health in the workplace; community organization; legal aid to the poor. Though this enlargement of the federal regulatory role was accompanied by marked growth in the size of government on all levels, the expansion has taken place primarily in state and local government. While the federal force increased by only 27 percent in the thirty years after 1950, the state and local government force increased by an astonishing 212 percent.

Despite the statistics, the conviction flourishes in some minds that the national government is a steadily growing behemoth swallowing up the liberties of the people. The foes of Washington prefer local government, feeling it is closer to the people and therefore allegedly more responsive to popular needs. Obviously there is a great deal to be said for settling local questions locally. But local government is characteristically the government of the locally powerful, whether planters, ranchers, merchants, bankers or industrialists. The way the locally powerless have found through our history to win their human and constitutional rights has very often been through appeal to the national government. The national government has vindicated racial justice against local bigotry, defended the Bill of Rights against local vigilantism, protected natural resources against local greed. It has civilized industry, secured the rights of labor organization, assured a steady income for the farmer. Had the states' rights creed prevailed, there would perhaps still be slavery in the United States.

The national authority, far from diminishing the individual, has given a majority of Americans more personal dignity and liberty than ever before. The individual freedoms destroyed by the increase in national authority have been in the main the freedom to deny black Americans their rights as citizens; the freedom to put small children to work in mills and immigrants in sweatshops; the freedom to pay starvation wages, require barbarous working hours, and permit squalid working conditions; the freedom to deceive in the sale of goods and securities; the freedom to pollute the environment—all freedoms that, one supposes, a civilized nation can readily do without.

"Statements are made," said President John F. Kennedy in 1963, "labelling the Federal Government an outsider, an intruder, an adversary. . . . The United States Government is not a stranger or not an enemy. It is the people of fifty states joining in a national effort. . . . Only a great national effort by a great people working together can explore the mysteries of space, harvest the products at the bottom of the ocean, and mobilize the human, natural, and material resources of our lands."

So an old debate continues. On one level of their minds the American people agree with Herbert Hoover and Ronald Reagan. On another we agree with Franklin Roosevelt and John Kennedy. When pollsters ask large, spacious questions—Do you think government has become too much involved in your lives? Do you think government should stop regulating business?—a sizable majority opposes

11

big government. But when asked specific questions about the practical work of government—Do you favor social security? unemployment compensation? Medicare? health and safety standards in factories? environmental protection? government guarantee of jobs for everyone seeking employment? price and wage controls when inflation threatens?—a sizable majority approves the intervention of the state.

All this expresses a disjunction in the American mind. Two eminent students of public opinion, Hadley Cantril and Lloyd A. Free, have drawn a distinction between the ideological and the operational spectrums in the realm of political belief. The ideological spectrum refers to attitudes toward government in the abstract; the operational spectrum to attitudes toward concrete programs affecting our daily lives. In 1967 Cantril and Free found that, while only 16 percent of us came out as liberals on the ideological spectrum, 65 percent came out as liberals on the operational spectrum—a discrepancy "so marked as to be almost schizoid." Polls do not display Americans measurably less schizoid on the subject of government today.

In general, Americans do not want less government. What they want is more efficient government. They want government to do a better job. For a time in the 1970s, with Vietnam, Watergate, and the Carter malaise, Americans lost confidence in the competence of the national government.. Asked "Can you trust government in Washington to do what is right?" over three quarters of those polled in 1964 had thought the national government could be trusted to do right most of the time. By 1980 only one quarter was prepared to offer such trust. But by 1984 trust in the capacity of the federal government to manage national affairs had climbed back to 45 percent. Ironically Ronald Reagan, the inveterate foe of government, has done much to restore the popular confidence in Washington.

Bureaucracy is a term of abuse. But bureaucracy is not peculiar to government. All large organizations are bureaucratic. It is impossible to run a large organization except through a division of labor and a hierarchy of authority. And we live in a world of large organizations. Without bureaucracy modern society, the private as well as the public sector, would collapse. The problem is not to abolish bureaucracy but to make it flexible, efficient and capable of innovation.

Two hundred years after the drafting of the Constitution Americans still regard government with a mixture of reliance and mistrust. This is not a bad combination. Mistrust is the best way to keep government reliable. Informed criticism is the means of correcting governmental inefficiency, incompetence, and arbitrariness; that is, of best enabling government to play its essential role. For we cannot do without government. "We the People of the United States," the preamble to the Constitution declares, formed our national government for compelling reasons—to "establish Justice, insure domestic Tranquility, provide for the common defence, promote the general Welfare, and secure the Blessings of Liberty to ourselves and our Posterity."

Without government, we cannot hope to attain the goals of the Founding Fathers. Without informed understanding of government, we cannot have the informed criticism that makes government do the job right. It is surely the duty of every American citizen to *Know Your Government*—which is what this series is all about.

New York
January, 1986

In the early morning hours of September 26, 1933, a small group of men surrounded a house in Memphis, Tennessee. Inside was George "Machine Gun" Kelly, who was wanted by the Federal Bureau of Investigation (FBI) for kidnapping. For two months, agents had trailed the gangster and his wife. The men of the FBI, accompanied by local police officers, quickly closed in around the house.

"We are federal officers. Come out with your hands up."

Machine Gun Kelly cowered in a corner. His trembling hands reached upward.

"Don't shoot, G-men! Don't shoot!"

This began a new name for FBI agents. By the time Kelly was convicted, the nickname, an abbreviation of "Government Men," had taken hold throughout the underworld. Along the grapevine of the powerful criminal empire, word spread about the feared "G-men."

George "Machine Gun" Kelly, the notorious thirties gangster who coined the term "G-man," was sentenced to life imprisonment for kidnapping.

1

Function of the Bureau

The Federal Bureau of Investigation is almost 80 years old. Its name is recognized by millions. To a great many, however, it is a mystery organization even though it is responsible for protecting our civil liberties and the security of the country. The FBI is the investigative and law enforcement branch of the U.S. Department of Justice. Its purpose is the enforcement of all federal criminal statutes, except for those specifically delegated to other federal agencies. Congress has authorized the Bureau to secure information, apprehend violators of federal laws, and to assist other law enforcement agencies, both state and local, with their missions. The results of FBI investigations are reported to the attorney general, the chief legal officer of the United States, who decides whether to prosecute. The FBI is supposed to report only the facts to those who determine government policy.

The responsibility of the FBI covers two main areas— general investigations of federal crimes and security operations. In the latter capacity, it is empowered to investigate

Six new posters join the "10 Most Wanted" list in the FBI building in 1970. The list, established in 1950, exceeded its 10-criminal limit during the rash of terrorism of the late 1960s and early 1970s.

espionage, sabotage, and any subversive activities that may affect the nation. The work of the Bureau is scrutinized by congressional committees, the Bureau of the Budget, and by the courts. As our society has become more complex, virtually every session of Congress has given the FBI new enforcement authority.

The FBI is not a national police force. However, it does help local police with their investigative work, particularly when a criminal act falls under both FBI and local jurisdiction. This includes bank robberies, as banks are insured by the federal government, and kidnapping in cases where the victim is taken across state lines. Of special value to local police is the

FBI's "Ten Most Wanted Fugitives" program, which gives nationwide publicity to those deemed the most dangerous criminals. Of all the suspects caught who appeared on this list, more than one-third have been identified by observant citizens who read the FBI "Most Wanted" posters, displayed in post offices and other public buildings.

The FBI Laboratory, established in 1932, has become the world's finest crime-detection laboratory. FBI scientists examine over 600,000 pieces of evidence yearly, including bullets, firearms, blood, hair, fibers, handwriting samples and tire prints.

FBI agents dust for fingerprints after a Manhattan bank robbery. Fingerprints, unique and unchanging for every individual, were first used to identify criminals by French criminologist Alphonse Bertillon (1853–1914).

Theodore Roosevelt (1858–1919), 26th president of the
United States, in cowboy garb. In the late 1880s he lived on
his ranch in Dakota territory. During his administration the
FBI was established in 1908.

2

Beginnings of the Bureau

The Fourth Amendment to the Constitution of the United States declares: "The right of the people to be secure in their persons, houses, papers, and effects against unreasonable searches and seizures shall not be violated." In establishing the Bureau in 1908, Congress was most conscious of this amendment and yet torn between individual freedoms and the increasing violations of federal laws. The congressional debates involving the new Bureau clearly show that the intent was not to establish a network of secret agents. And yet, something had to be done about the alarming rise in national crime. Congress interpreted the "commerce clause" of the Constitution—the clause that authorizes Congress to regulate commerce between the states—as allowing federal jurisdiction over interstate crime. And so, the Bureau of Investigation was established. In 1935, Congress changed the name to the Federal Bureau of Investigation.

The Bureau's duties and responsibilities originally were ill-defined. Matters placed under its jurisdiction included trea-

President Woodrow Wilson (1856–1924) prepares to draw the first capsule in a World War I draft lottery. During his administration military service was made compulsory, and apprehension of draft evaders was designated the responsibility of the FBI.

son, crime on the high seas, crimes committed on Indian reservations, opium smuggling, impersonation of a federal officer, fraudulent bankruptcies, and violations of the anti-trust laws. The Bureau started with fewer than 60 agents, mainly political appointees.

The growth of federal laws since 1908 has resulted in a corresponding broadening of the FBI's authority. The small organization gradually expanded. The Mann Act (1910), for example, made it illegal to transport women across state lines for immoral purposes. Enforcement of this act fell to the Bureau. The Selective Service Act (1917) and the apprehension of draft evaders, as well as new espionage laws to block the work of spies, brought new duties to the organization. The National Motor Vehicle Theft Act (1919) gave the Bureau authority to curb the increasing transportation of stolen automobiles from state to state.

In spite of its increased responsibilities, the Bureau was woefully unprepared to handle espionage and saboteurs during World War I. The German ambassador to the United States, for example, had organized a highly efficient espionage ring. One of its more successful exploits destroyed a federal arms and ammunition depot on Black Tom Island in New York Harbor on July 30, 1916. The thunderous noise reverberated for 100 miles. The concussion shattered almost every window in Jersey City and heavy plate glass windows crashed to the sidewalk of Manhattan. Black Tom's usefulness had been destroyed.

After the United States entered the war in 1917, Congress—at the urging of President Woodrow Wilson—passed laws that established compulsory military service, limited the rights of aliens, and restricted freedom of speech and the press. These laws created additional duties for the Bureau, which was now responsible for the apprehension of draft evaders and individuals suspected of espionage, treason, or sedition. Also in 1917, a young lawyer named J. Edgar Hoover, who would profoundly affect the organization's future, joined the Justice Department.

War hysteria swept the nation. Violent changes occurred both at home and abroad. The Russian Revolution (1917) toppled the centuries-old tsarist monarchy, bringing Lenin and the Communist party to power. Against this backdrop of successful

Members of the Ku Klux Klan parade down Pennsylvania Avenue in Washington, D.C., in 1925. During this period the General Intelligence Division of the Bureau probed into the workings of the organization and weakened its power.

German sabotage, war hysteria, and fears of an international Communist revolution, maintenance of internal security became the primary mission of the Bureau.

Unfortunately, the Bureau's eager but relatively untrained staff often violated the civil liberties of individuals through illegal detentions and spying. These violations, explained away as essential for the survival of the nation, included investigations of personal beliefs that the Bureau considered harmful to the war effort.

Alleged subversives were arrested for disagreeing with the government's war objectives. The civil rights of aliens were sharply curtailed, and many American citizens found themselves detained because of their personal opinions and associations. Government agencies opened private letters and seized certain magazines and newspapers as evidence of disloyalty. Government officials viewed dissent as treasonous—and the Bureau of Investigation stood at the forefront of checking political thought.

Volunteer organizations who wanted to help the war effort committed the worst excesses. One group, the American Protective League (APL), with Bureau blessing, gathered information about suspected draft evaders and possible saboteurs. But many APL members, in their patriotic zeal, made illegal citizen arrests and conducted unlawful searches. In many cases, APL members encouraged the impression that they were federal officers. Labor leaders bitterly protested that the League intimidated strikers exercising their constitutional rights. Even President Wilson spoke out against "the great danger of citizens taking the law into their own hands." The APL was finally disbanded in 1919.

The First World War (1914–1918) accelerated the change in America from a rural to an industrial society. But the nerves of the country had been rubbed raw by the bitterness over the war, the protracted debate on the League of Nations, the Red Scare and the postwar inflation. Americans continued to be suspicious of foreigners, frightened at the prospect of Communist conspiracies, and wary of new or different ideas that challenged traditional authority. These years saw violent labor

Following World War I, American society began to experience the growing pains of rapid industrialization. Industrial laborers organized strikes in an effort to secure better working conditions and higher wages.

strikes, many of them spearheaded by the Industrial Workers of the World (IWW), a militant labor union whose members were commonly called "Wobblies." The IWW advocated worker control of mines and factories. To many, these goals seemed too similar to those espoused by revolutionary Communist parties.

The year 1919 saw a sudden spate of bombs directed against prominent government officials and financiers. Although the intended targets escaped almost unharmed, the bombings caused a great deal of material damage. A nation panicked, and the IWW and the Communists received the blame. Then, in 1920, a bomb exploded in New York, near the Wall Street offices of J. P. Morgan, a banker who symbolized the capitalist system. This time, thirty-three people died, mostly passersby, and over 300 were injured. No one ever discovered who set the bomb.

Would Communist revolutions spread to other nations? Would the United States be engulfed in a class war? In 1919, the Bureau established a new General Intelligence Division to war against radicals. Its head, 24-year-old J. Edgar Hoover, warned that the "present organized world-wide class struggle threatens the foundations of society and civilization itself" and that radicals "threaten the happiness of the community, the safety of every individual, and the continuance of every home

Rubble and confused masses filled the street after the Wall Street explosion of 1920. The bombing was one of a spate of subversive acts directed against prominent government officials and financiers in New York City.

and fireside. They would destroy the peace of the country and thrust it into a condition of anarchy and lawlessness and immorality that pass imagination."

Alarmed about the perceived threat to national security, the United States Senate urged Attorney General A. Mitchell Palmer to do something—and fast. The attorney general launched the infamous Palmer's "Red Raids" (1919–20). These raids involved mass arrests of political and labor agitators, often on the flimsiest of evidence. If those arrested were not native-born Americans, even if they had obtained citizenship through naturalization, they still faced almost certain deportation. Perhaps the most famous to be expelled from the country were the noted anarchists Emma Goldman and Alexander Berkman. Young Edgar Hoover assisted the government prosecutors in their case by preparing a legal brief which asserted that, since the Soviet Union controlled the American Communist Party, any citizen belonging to the party could be legally treated as an alien and deported.

In his zeal to protect the nation from unorthodox political views, Hoover began compiling files on every alleged extremist living in the United States—that is, of every person believed by his agents to hold what the Bureau considered dangerous ideas. Within a month, this index contained the names of 100,000 "radicals"; within a year it held 450,000 names. In addition, Hoover directed his staff to write biographies of the more important activists. By mid-1920, the General Intelligence Division had compiled biographies of over 60,000 so-called radicals. These files were to be used in case a national emergency required immediate detention of subversives.

In defense of these activities, Hoover wrote, "Freedom of speech is always a liberty but never a license." He claimed: "Never upon any occasion has the department wavered from the traditional American position which holds free speech and opinion, where law abiding, the most cherished of our inalienable rights."

Russian-born anarchist Alexander Berkman (1870–1936) addresses a New York City rally of the Industrial Workers of the World (IWW). Imprisoned for the attempted assassination of industrialist Henry Frick, Berkman was arrested and deported during the Palmer "Red Raids."

Ku Klux Klan activity is under constant FBI surveillance. Here an FBI agent displays an arsenal and assorted Klan paraphernalia confiscated from the homes of six individuals charged with conspiring to bomb ten Michigan school buses in 1971 to protest against school integration.

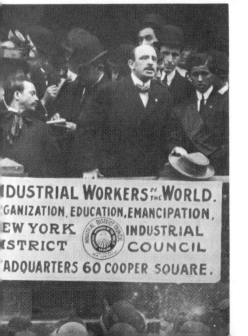

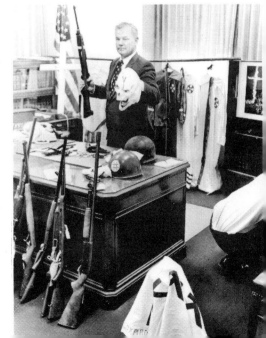

When the Warren G. Harding administration came into office in 1921, Hoover, at age 26, was designated assistant director of the Bureau of Investigation. President Harding made some able appointments, but he also brought with him his small-town "Ohio gang," which proceeded to make a shambles of his administration. Soon scandals involving high government officials shook Washington. Even Attorney General Harry Daugherty (1921–24) illegally sold liquor permits, as well as pardons and paroles to criminals. (Two divided, or "hung," juries in 1926 enabled him to escape a prison sentence.)

Under Daugherty, the Bureau of Investigation became a political tool. Agents got their jobs through their friendships with senators and congressmen. The Bureau was used for confidential investigations of people and matters of interest to Daugherty. Agents spied on members of Congress who had demanded investigations of reported corruption in the administration. They opened congressional mail and searched personal office files to find damaging material that could be used to stop congressional attacks on the attorney general. Hoover later wrote that he came close to resigning in disgust during this period. Harding seemed overwhelmed when these spectacular scandals involving Daugherty and other appointees began to surface. The president died in office on August 2, 1923, and was succeeded by Calvin Coolidge.

President Coolidge fired Daugherty and appointed Harlan Fiske Stone, the former dean of the Columbia University School of Law, as his attorney general (1924–25). (Less than a year later, Coolidge appointed Stone to be associate justice of the Supreme Court, and in 1941 President Roosevelt made him chief justice.) Stone's assignment was to clean up the Justice Department, particularly the Bureau of Investigation.

On May 10, 1924, Attorney General Stone chose 29-year-old J. Edgar Hoover to be the head of the Bureau. Hoover recalled the conversation:

"I'll take the job, Mr. Stone, on certain conditions."

"What are they?"

"The Bureau must be divorced from politics and not be a catch-all for political hacks. Appointments must be based on merit. Second, promotions will be made on proved ability and the Bureau will be responsible only to the attorney general."

The attorney general replied, "I wouldn't give it to you under any other conditions. That's all. Good day."

The old order had ended.

Attorney General Harry M. Daugherty on the steps of the White House. President Calvin Coolidge promptly requested Daugherty's resignation in 1924 when it became known that he had repeatedly used the FBI to further his own political interests.

A. Mitchell Palmer (1872–1936), who was appointed U.S. attorney general by President Woodrow Wilson conducted massive raids with the FBI against suspected subversives. Palmer had supported Wilson at the 1912 Democratic convention in Baltimore.

Attorney General Harlan Fiske Stone (1872–1946) restored public confidence lost by his predecessor, Harry M. Daugherty, a President Harding appointee, to the office of attorney general. Later, as chief justice of the United States, Stone, a liberal Republican, upheld many New Deal policies.

Four-year-old J. Edgar Hoover (1895–1972). Among his many personal trademarks were his impeccable appearance and his machine-gun-like manner of speech, which earned him the nickname "Speed" among his classmates.

3

J. Edgar Hoover

J. Edgar Hoover was one of a kind, certainly one of the most distinctive individuals ever to head a governmental agency in United States history. He served as director of the FBI for nearly half a century under eight presidents and sixteen attorneys general. He built the Bureau into a dominant and, at times, controversial force in American law enforcement. The FBI became so strongly identified with Hoover that he himself became a national institution. No other federal agency ever became so closely identified with a single personality as did the Bureau.

John Edgar Hoover was born in Washington, D.C., on New Year's Day, 1895. His birthplace is commemorated by a stained-glass window in the Presbyterian church that now stands on the site of the house where he spent his youth. As a boy, Hoover was known as "Speed," apparently a reference to his fast and clipped manner of speech. Valedictorian of his high school class, he was described in his yearbook as "a gentleman of dauntless courage and stainless honor." The University of Virginia offered him a full-tuition scholarship, but Hoover feared that living expenses there would burden his father. Instead, he took a $30-a-month job as a clerk in the Library of Congress and enrolled in the George Washington University night school. After receiving his law degree from the university and passing the bar exam in 1917, Hoover moved to a $1200-a-year job with the Department of Justice—his employer for the next 55 years.

From the start, according to a 1937 profile of Hoover in *The New Yorker* magazine, he stood out from the other young lawyers around him:

> He dressed better than most, a bit on the dandyish side. He had exceptional capacity for detail work, and he handled small chores with enthusiasm and thoughtfulness. He constantly sought new responsibilities to shoulder, and welcomed chances to work overtime. When he was in conference with an official of his department, his manner was that of a young man who confidently expected to rise.

One of Hoover's first positions in the Department of Justice was as head of the General Intelligence Division, working to counter radical activities. Changes brought by World War I, especially the Communist revolution in Russia, led to a fear that radical revolutions would spread. Although American radicals and leftist groups, such as the Socialists, had split over the virtues of the new Soviet government, most people viewed it as a dictatorship. And even though the total number of Communists in the United States probably comprised less than one-half of 1 percent of the population, public fear of the "Red menace" grew.

Violence in labor disputes after the war also deepened concern over public safety. In 1919 alone, 3,630 strikes involved more than 4 million workers who sought higher wages to keep up with the cost of living, which soared after wartime controls had ended. Strikes became identified with subversion and dangerous foreign ideas. Communist agitators were blamed for a strike in September 1919 against United States Steel Corporation plants. Numerous bomb scares and actual bombings deepened the fear that a massive radical conspiracy planned to overthrow the United States government. Attorney General A. Mitchell Palmer declared: "like a prairie fire, the blaze of revolution was sweeping over every American institution." He

Emma Goldman (1869–1940), Lithuanian-born U.S. anarchist and labor agitator. She and fellow anarchist Alexander Berkman served two years in prison for opposing the draft. Shortly after their release they were deported to the Soviet Union.

Palmer "Red Raid" victims board a steamer to Ellis Island in 1920 prior to their deportation. One of the largest raids occurred on January 2, 1920, when government agents in 33 cities took 2,700 people into custody.

J. Edgar Hoover (center) on a 1938 trip to Florida with FBI special agent Guy Hottell (left) and Clyde Tolson (right). Tolson joined the Bureau in 1928.

wrote that the "sharp tongues of the Revolution's head were licking the altars of the churches, leaping into the belfry of the school bell, crawling into the sacred corners of American homes, and seeking to replace marriage vows with libertine laws."

As the head of the newly formed General Intelligence Division, Hoover built up an information system that was used against the radicals. These files, preserved today in the National Archives, the U.S. government's record-keeping center in Washington, clearly illustrate the way in which unsubstantiated information was used against individuals, often in complete disregard of their legal rights. Many years later, Hoover deplored the hysteria that led to the arrests and deportation of innocent aliens in 1919 and 1920, but the records show that he personally planned and executed numerous campaigns against blameless individuals whom he suspected of being disloyal.

Hoover became the Bureau chief in 1924. For the next 48 years J. Edgar Hoover was "Mr. FBI," the symbol of law enforcement, the indomitable G-Man. Under his leadership, the FBI developed a reputation for integrity and freedom from political control, although it was subject to criticism for its methods, particularly during Hoover's later years as director. His power was based on a shrewd combination of perfomance and politics, publicity, and personality. He made speeches and wrote volumes on the enemies of law and order. He portrayed himself as the nation's foremost bulwark against evil, both foreign and domestic.

By the end of his first 15 years in office, Hoover had indeed established an extraordinary record of innovation in law enforcement. Among his many achievements were the establishment of training schools to teach special agents modern crime detection methods; the creation of a centralized fingerprint file (now containing more than 200 million prints); the construction of state-of-the-art crime laboratories; the founding of the National Police Academy (formed in 1935 to train local police in the detection of crimes); the recruitment of lawyers and accountants as special agents; and the creation of the National Crime Information Center, which enables more than 4,000 local law enforcement agencies to use a centralized computer data base.

When Hoover died, at age 77, on May 2, 1972, his flag-draped coffin was placed on Abraham Lincoln's catafalque in

FBI agents positively matched the shoes of a woman's alleged assailant to heel-prints found at the scene of the crime, leading to a conviction. Gathering evidence of this kind is an arduous task requiring patience and close attention to detail.

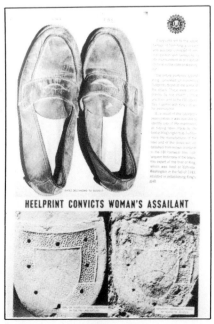

HEELPRINT CONVICTS WOMAN'S ASSAILANT

the Capitol Rotunda, the first time such an honor had been accorded to a civil servant. The Rotunda remained open all night, with the presidential honor guard changing watch every 30 minutes. High government officials crowded into the chamber to pay their respects. Tributes came from all over the nation. The Boys Clubs of America announced the establishment of a J. Edgar Hoover Freedom Award to perpetuate the late FBI director's "memory and his inspiration to millions of American boys." The chief justice of the United States, Warren Burger, delivered the eulogy and praised "this splendid man who dedicated his life to his country in a half-century of unparalleled service. . . . He has justly been and will be an American legend." And, public opinion seemed to agree with the chief justice. A Gallup Poll completed shortly before Hoover's death showed that an unprecedented 80 percent of those who had any opinion of Hoover rated his performance "good" or "excellent."

But there was another side to J. Edgar Hoover—the side that became more evident in his later years in office. By the 1970s, Hoover was frequently under public criticism for what some called his authoritarian administration of the Bureau. So great was his prestige, however, that no president dared to remove him. As the nation's fears shifted from radicals and Reds in the 1920s; to gangsters in the 1930s; to Nazi saboteurs in the 1940s; to Communists in the 1950s; and to civil rights, peace demonstrators, and campus radicals in the 1960s and 1970s, J. Edgar Hoover's ultra-conservative philosophy often provided him with an excuse to overlook the guarantees of freedom as enunciated in the Bill of Rights.

Throughout his years as FBI director, J. Edgar Hoover projected two entirely different images. One was that of the heroic G-Man who triumphed over crooks and subversives— the other of a secret police chief working to crush political and social change. In retrospect, perhaps the career of J. Edgar Hoover was far less melodramatic than he often made it appear and far more significant than he realized. Both Hoover and the FBI reflected the growth and complexities of federal law and of how these laws affected American society.

J. Edgar Hoover in 1928. The FBI director, a lifelong bachelor, lived with his mother until her death in 1938. That year he moved from the home where he grew up to his own house in the Northwest section of Washington, D.C.

The vastness of government documentation is shown by this view of the FBI identification division, where 65 million fingerprints are kept on file. This Bureau division was established in 1924 with more than 800,000 fingerprints collected from local police chiefs and the federal penitentiary in Leavenworth, Kansas.

WANTED

JOHN HERBERT DILLINGER

On June 23, 1934, HOMER S. CUMMINGS, Attorney General of the United States, under the authority vested in him by an Act of Congress approved June 6, 1934, offered a reward of

$10,000.00

for the capture of John Herbert Dillinger or a reward of

$5,000.00

for information leading to the arrest of John Herbert Dillinger.

DESCRIPTION

Age, 32 years; Height, 5 feet 7-1/8 inches; Weight, 153 pounds; Build, medium; Hair, medium chestnut; Eyes, grey; Complexion, medium; Occupation, machinist; Marks and scars, 1/2 inch scar back left hand, scar middle upper lip, brown mole between eyebrows.

All claims to any of the aforesaid rewards and all questions and disputes that may arise as among claimants to the foregoing rewards shall be passed upon by the Attorney General and his decisions shall be final and conclusive. The right is reserved to divide and allocate portions of any of said rewards as between several claimants. No part of the aforesaid rewards shall be paid to any official or employee of the Department of Justice.

If you are in possession of any information concerning the whereabouts of John Herbert Dillinger, communicate immediately by telephone or telegraph collect to the nearest office of the Division of Investigation, United States Department of Justice, the local addresses of which are set forth on the reverse side of this notice.

JOHN EDGAR HOOVER, DIRECTOR,
DIVISION OF INVESTIGATION,
UNITED STATES DEPARTMENT OF JUSTICE,
WASHINGTON, D. C.

June 25, 1934

A John Dillinger wanted poster issued in 1934, bearing his description and the offer of a reward for information leading to his arrest. The FBI continues to display posters such as this one in post offices and other government buildings across the country to alert the public to criminals at large.

4

The
Gangster Era

The 1920s and 1930s stand as a high point in the history of American crime. Criminals had better weapons and faster automobiles than the agencies that were supposed to stop them. They held enormous influence over many local police forces. Gangsters had created their own empires through alliances with crooked politicians, lawyers, and policemen. Vast fortunes were made from bootleg liquor, prostitution, gambling, narcotics, and protection schemes. The yearly income of the Chicago mob at its peak of power exceeded $300 million.

Ironically, it may well have been that the greatest impetus to the new wave of crime was the Eighteenth Amendment to the Constitution, adopted in 1919, which made the drinking and selling of alcoholic beverages illegal. But millions of Americans scorned Prohibition, as the amendment was known, and a veritable army of bootleggers catered to a thirsty nation by providing illegal liquor, wine, and beer. Ships from Europe and Latin America carrying contraband goods would anchor outside the U.S. three-mile limit as they were unloaded by rumrunners—operators of high-powered boats—who would then try to slip past Coast Guard patrols. Sometimes they had to fight their way through. Bootlegging was a dangerous profession but its profits were enormous. A $15 case of whiskey could be sold for as much as $80; a $3 barrel of beer for $60. At one point during Prohibition, ships anchored off New Jersey contained an estimated $225 million worth of whiskey. Bribery of enforcement officials was common. A policeman earning $44 a week, for example, could get several hundred dollars just for looking the other way.

In 1929, the U.S. assistant attorney general, who was in charge of Prohibition enforcement, conceded that liquor could be bought at almost any hour of the day or night any place in America. J. Edgar Hoover accurately described the situation when he wrote: "American law enforcement had reached a crisis. . . . Men and women who had engaged in every form of outlawing—even to mass murder—were assembled under a common banner, with the result that great numbers of criminals were ready and eager to take up new forms of lawbreaking of the most vicious sort."

One of the most publicized of these outlaw groups was the unlikely duo of Bonnie Parker and Clyde Barrow. In a wave of small-time crime, they held up grocery stores and filling

stations rather than large banks—but between 1930 and 1934 they killed 13 persons during their escapades. The two were among the most hunted criminals. Members of the Texas Highway Patrol, tipped off by an informant, killed Bonnie and Clyde in a bloody 1934 shootout.

President Herbert Hoover, appalled at rising crime statistics, appointed a National Committee on Law Observance and Enforcement in 1929 to recommend ways of handling the growing problem. Two years later, the committee published its findings in a document known as the Wickersham Report, named for its chairman, former Attorney General George Wickersham. The report emphasized the national character of crime and the lack of effective law enforcement. For the cleanup, Congress turned to the FBI. At this time, the Bureau had only 266 special agents.

On March 1, 1932, the son of the famed aviator Charles Lindbergh was kidnapped from his New Jersey home. Lindbergh, the first person to fly solo across the Atlantic, had become an international hero, and the crime shocked the entire world. The kidnapper demanded $50,000 in ransom, and the money was paid. Seventy-two days later, searchers found the child's body in a desolate wooded area four-and-one-half miles from the Lindbergh home. A blow had crushed his skull. The nation was horrified. Perhaps no other crime had evoked such

Faye Dunaway and Warren Beatty, in the 1967 film *Bonnie and Clyde* (right), strike a pose similar to that of the actual bandit couple (left). Bonnie and Clyde sent pictures of themselves to the nation's newspapers, which eagerly printed them.

Customs agents unload bootleg liquor in New York City (1930). Prohibition was flagrantly violated from its inception. Saloons reopened as speakeasies and bootlegging became a vast business enterprise. For a price, many officials, such as Chicago Mayor William H. Thompson, condoned the liquor rackets.

anger. Congress rushed to pass the Federal Kidnapping Statute (1932), known as the Lindbergh Law, which made it a federal crime to transport a kidnap victim across a state line and provided the death penalty for conviction.

The Lindbergh investigation developed into a cooperative effort among the New Jersey state police, the New York City police department, and the FBI. The first real lead in the case occurred on September 15, 1934, when a motorist paid for five gallons of gasoline at a Bronx, New York, filling station with a $10 gold certificate. The attendant, suspicious because these notes had been recalled in 1933 when the United States went off the gold standard, wrote the license number of the car on the certificate. Three days later, a bank teller spotted the certificate as one of the marked bills used to pay the Lindbergh ransom. The FBI was notified. They traced the license number of the car to Bruno Hauptmann, an unemployed carpenter, and he was arrested. Additional ransom money was found in his pocket. Evidence piled up, and, after a sensational trial, Hauptmann died in the electric chair on April 3, 1936, for the murder of the Lindbergh boy.

Although the FBI had no jurisdiction over the case because the child had not been transported over a state line, its crime laboratories had amassed the needed evidence against the kidnapper and turned it over to local authorities. The work of the Bureau enabled the state of New Jersey to prosecute the crime successfully.

Throughout the late 1920s and into the 1930s, the FBI developed progressively more sophisticated crime-fighting techniques. The public was fascinated by real-life crime stories involving FBI agents. Police departments across the country were so impressed by the Bureau's brilliant detection work in solving kidnappings and bank robberies and in destroying criminal gangs that police chiefs and local law enforcement officers began to attend the FBI Academy to learn the latest methods of apprehending criminals. They took such courses as "Chemistry in Crime Detection" and the "Study of Blood and Hair in Solving Crime." It was new scientific methods of detection, taught to these local enforcement agents, that helped end the era of lawlessness.

The 1930s were indeed vintage years for gangsters. Perhaps the most publicized case of the era was J. Edgar Hoover's personal arrest of Alvin Karpis, one of the last surviving big-name criminals of the gangster era.

Karpis grew up in Topeka, Kansas. As a teenager, he rifled cash registers in local candy and grocery stores. As he grew

A bystander desperately tries to collect some precious banned liquor in his hat as a federal agent empties bottles in 1933. Prohibition, known as the "noble experiment" but marked by bootleggers, illegal speakeasies, and violent crimes, ended in December 1933 when the 18th Amendment was repealed.

more brazen, he robbed a jewelry shop and was caught. Sentenced to ten years in the state prison, he managed to escape after two. Mobsters nicknamed him "Old Creepy" because his fish-eyed stare made them shudder. He went to Tulsa, Oklahoma, and, in 1931, joined forces with Arthur "Doc" Barker in a major criminal career. Assisting them were Doc Barker's three brothers, Herman, Fred, and Lloyd. But the mastermind of the gang was the mother of the Barker boys, Kate Barker. From her appearance, no one would have suspected that this fat, pleasant-looking woman, known as Ma Barker, had trained her four sons to be robbers, kidnappers, and murderers. She planned the robberies and the getaways. When a robbery was over, she hid those who took part in it. If any of the 20 or so members of her gang were caught, she hired lawyers to defend them. If they escaped from prison, she provided a secure hideout. Anyone who crossed the Barker-Karpis mob courted death.

Ma Barker's lover, suspected of unfaithfulness, was taken for a typical gangland "ride." Police found his horribly mutilated body by the shore of a lake with a woman's bloodstained glove beside him as a memento of his fatal love affair. Although the police and the FBI believed Ma Barker to be responsible for at least a hundred robberies, she had never spent one day in jail. Alvin Karpis joined this gang. He soon became Ma Barker's number two man.

Between 1931 and 1936, the Barker-Karpis band of malcontents killed at least ten people and stole more than $1 million. The gang, made up of paroled convicts, often found hiding

Public Enemy Number One Alvin "Creepy" Karpis arrives for questioning at a federal building in St. Paul, Minnesota, in 1936. Having received threatening letters from Karpis, Hoover (in foreground) made a point of arresting the man himself.

places in towns where local police conveniently did not recognize them.

After Doc Barker and Karpis killed a sheriff in Missouri, the police of the entire country hunted for them. Ma moved operations to St. Paul, Minnesota, where she and Karpis decided to kidnap one of the city's wealthiest citizens. In January 1934 the gang abducted Edward Bremer, president of the Commercial State Bank of St. Paul, held him prisoner for almost a month, and released him after collecting $200,000 in $5 and $10 bills.

With the ransom paid and the victim safe, the FBI now closed in. Through clever work, detectives found a fingerprint of Doc Barker, and a local salesclerk identified Karpis. As the fugitives passed the marked ransom, FBI agents followed the trail to Lake Weir, Florida. In 1935, with the hideout located,

Charles Lindbergh (1902–1974), whose heroic solo flight across the Atlantic in 1927 made him one of the best-loved Americans of his era. The 1932 kidnapping and murder of his first child was a major case for the FBI.

Charles "Pretty Boy" Floyd became Public Enemy Number One after Dillinger's death. Floyd eluded capture numerous times, and his exploits were much sensationalized. He was killed in a shootout with FBI agents in Ohio in 1934.

FBI agents demanded that its occupants surrender. The answer—a burst of machine-gun fire. A pitched battle followed. The agents hurled tear gas bombs, and riddled the cottage until the Barkers' guns appeared silenced. Ma Barker and her son Fred had been killed. Most of the ransom money was found buried near the house. But Karpis escaped the dragnet. (Of the other three sons of Ma Barker, Herman committed suicide in 1927 rather than face arrest, and Arthur died in 1939 while trying to escape from Alcatraz prison. Lloyd was killed by his wife in 1949.)

The capture of Karpis became paramount for Hoover. On April 24, 1935, Karpis and two heavily armed confederates held up a mail truck in Ohio and escaped with $70,000. Shortly afterward, the gang raided a train bound from Detroit to Pittsburgh, seized more than $30,000, and escaped in a waiting airplane.

Karpis brazenly sent word to Hoover that he would personally kill him just as FBI agents had killed Ma Barker and her son. Hoover ordered his agents to give him any information they received on Karpis's whereabouts. FBI agents knew that Public Enemy No. 1 was "the Boss's man."

Dozens of FBI agents finally traced Karpis to New Orleans. On May 1, 1936, Hoover, leading his agents, captured Alvin Karpis. "With necessary reinforcements for the raiding party," Hoover later wrote, "we swooped down out of the sky after an all-night airplane ride from Washington. . . . "The FBI men drove to Karpis's hideout. Hoover recalled, " 'Put the cuffs on him, boys,' I said. Then it developed that not one of us had a pair of handcuffs. They were in the other cars. A crowd was gathering and we had to move fast, so the two agents bound the hands of the hoodlum with their neckties." Although the final apprehension may have been less than perfect, the result was that Hoover had personally made an important arrest. His popularity soared.

Undoubtedly, the most notorious criminal of the 1930s was John Dillinger. After being jailed for murdering a policeman, Dillinger escaped and led a gang on a crime spree through the Midwest from September 1933 until July 1934. They left a

44

trail of ten people murdered, seven seriously wounded, four banks robbed, and three police arsenals plundered. The subject of numerous exhibits at the FBI Museum in Washington and of countless articles written by Hoover and by writers to whom he supplied material, Dillinger easily rates as the number one criminal in the history of the FBI. The entire nation talked

John Dillinger's collection of weapons, confiscated by the FBI, included two Thompson submachine guns. A favorite of gangsters and FBI agents alike, the "Tommy" gun became a symbol of the gangster era. Hoover removed the weapon from the FBI arsenal in 1969.

By far the number one criminal in the history of the FBI, John Dillinger (in shirtsleeves) sits surrounded by guards at a hearing on charges of shooting an Indiana policeman.

about Dillinger's exploits and his daring criminal rampage.

FBI agents came close to capturing Dillinger and his gang several times, but the resourceful criminals always managed to escape. Finally, on July 21, 1934, the madam of a Gary, Indiana, brothel informed FBI agents that Dillinger planned to take her to the movies the following evening. She told them they could identify her by the bright red dress she would wear. At the Biograph Theater in Chicago the next evening, agents closed in around "the lady in red" and her companion. Ignoring a command to surrender, Dillinger whipped out his gun and headed for an alley. Other agents had already closed it off but Dillinger was determined to shoot it out. He fell at last in the gutter, making good his boast that he "would never be taken alive."

Some newspapers and magazines, competing for higher circulation figures, tried to glorify the Dillinger gang and other criminals of the day. Hoover repeatedly spoke out against what he called those "sob-sisters" and "sentimental yammerheads." The FBI chief appeared before civic and religious groups to denounce not only criminals but attempts to romanticize their exploits. He inspired young people to strive for the highest moral values. In fact, Hoover encouraged the magazines of the 1930s, and the Hearst publications in particular, to carry comic strips and stories portraying the FBI in a favorable way, stressing the theme that crime does not pay.

Hoover used the media to promote a positive image of the FBI. He gradually built legends about agents involved in wild shootouts with thugs, reminiscent of the old frontier. He promoted "junior G-Man" clubs for boys. His own book, *Masters of Deceit* (1958), sold almost three million copies. In 1965, he personally selected the actor (Efrem Zimbalist, Jr.) who would represent the FBI in a popular television series.

The disciplined men around Hoover accepted the FBI policy of anonymity—and the Chief alone served as its spokesman as well as the person in America most associated with crime busting. Hoover took much of the credit for successful operations, always personally announcing sensational arrests of criminals. Annual reports of the FBI gave the impression that the Bureau, single-handedly, was wiping out crime. Newspapers headlined FBI exploits. Thousands of tourists who visited the FBI headquarters viewed exhibits that made the director into a Dick Tracy-type figure, one who was always close on the heels of the lawbreaker. By the end of the 1930s, J. Edgar Hoover was, after the president of the United States, the most popular man in America.

George "Baby Face" Nelson took turns with "Pretty Boy" Floyd for the Public Enemy Number One spot after Dillinger's death. Nelson's first arrest was for stealing automobile parts when he was 13.

Philip Abbott, Efrem Zimbalist, Jr., and Stephen Brooks played agents on the television series *The FBI*. Bureau staff went over every script for the series to ensure that the plots were realistic.

The kingpin of the gangster era, Al Capone. Seeking refuge from the constant chase of his enemies, "Scarface" turned himself in to Philadelphia authorities in 1929. He was convicted of income tax evasion in 1931.

5

Organized Crime

$\mathbf{I}$n the 1920s, the age of bathtub gin, speakeasies, and flappers, perhaps no other gangster so typified the era as did Al Capone. The man known as "Scarface" started as a rough street thug in Brooklyn with a gang run by a bootlegger, Johnny Torrio. When Torrio moved to Chicago in 1920 he took Capone with him. Capone rose quickly in Torrio's criminal organization, and he was largely responsible for its success. In the bloody mob warfare, Torrio was so badly injured that he retired from the rackets in 1925, leaving Capone to take charge.

In Chicago, a city infamous for its gangsterism and racketeering (In one 30-month period from 1924–1926, Chicago had 92 reported gang murders), Capone became the most powerful crime boss of the day. He not only dominated illegal rackets such as liquor, gambling, and prostitution, but through bribery and graft controlled most of the police force, numerous politicians, and many judges. Businessmen were forced to buy "protection," and many labor unions fell into the hands of

A sawed-off shotgun (pictured) or a Tommy gun in a violin case became symbolic of mob warfare. Gangsters, in movies as well as real life, became part of American mythology during the 1930s.

Chorus girls do the Charleston, a popular dance of the Roaring Twenties, or Jazz Age, the decade of Prohibition. In a time of wild abandon and riotous pleasure-seeking, the FBI sought to enforce Prohibition laws and curb racketeering.

hoodlums. In an attempt to wipe out one of the last rival gangs, headed by George "Bugs" Moran, Capone ordered the 1929 "St. Valentine's Day Massacre," in which seven men were machine-gunned in a garage. This bloodbath so revolted the public that law enforcement officials were finally forced to take action to curb the excesses of the bootleg wars. By 1926, homicides in the United States reached the alarming number of 12,000 a year.

Although the FBI charged Capone with a few minor offenses, it was the Internal Revenue Service that finally brought him down. He was convicted of income tax evasion in 1931 and sentenced to 11 years in prison. Released in 1939 because of ill health, Capone died at his Florida estate in 1947.

Capone left an enduring legacy to organized crime. One of his talents had been an ability to consolidate criminal factions. He had merged the Camorra gang (a mob whose mem-

Lucky Luciano in 1957. Luciano, nicknamed "Charlie Lucky" because he miraculously survived a gangland "ride" in his early criminal days, was arrested 25 times in the United States and was finally deported to Italy in 1946, never to return.

Meyer Lansky, reputed financial genius of the underworld, outside a Manhattan courtroom in 1958. Once boasting to an associate that organized crime was "bigger than U.S. Steel," Lansky directed mob enterprises such as bootlegging, gambling, loan sharking, stock manipulation and penetration into legitimate businesses.

bers were of Neapolitan background) with the rival Mafia (its Sicilian counterpart), forming a group that later came to be known as *La Cosa Nostra* (Italian for "Our Thing"). Thus Capone's work in the 1920s laid the foundation for a national crime syndicate in the following decade.

Based on traditions that date back to the 16th century, the Mafia and the Camorra emerged in poverty-stricken Italy during the mid-1800s. In that period, law in Italy was weak and poorly enforced. The landed gentry brutally exploited the poorer classes, hiring bullies to impose restrictions and collect rents. Eventually, these ruffians banded together and became so powerful that they turned against the landowners themselves. They dictated to their former employers whom to hire and what to pay them, and they fixed the prices of the rents and crops.

Some members of the Mafia came to the United States from Europe in the late 19th and early 20th centuries with the great influx of immigrants who arrived in this country during those years. They plunged into bootlegging during Prohibition. At first the organization was threatened by brutal infighting among its various factions, but in 1931 New York crime lord Salvatore Maranzano organized the crime syndicate in major cities, dividing it into "families," each of which ran a combi-

The bullet-riddled body of Albert Anastasia in the barber shop of the Park Sheraton Hotel in Manhattan in 1957. Anastasia, known as "The Executioner" for his leadership of Murder, Inc., was implicated in 31 gangland killings, but his only murder conviction was overturned when four prosecution witnesses disappeared before his retrial.

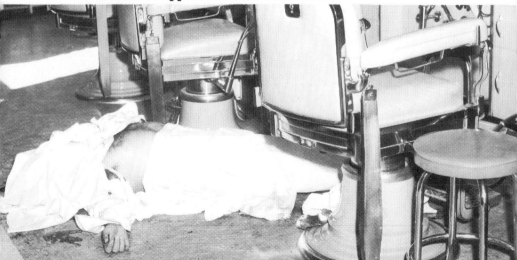

Movie actor George Raft and his gangster pal, Benjamin "Bugsy" Siegel (left) in 1944. Siegel began his criminal career in New York during the early 1930s, but later moved west. He mixed with many Hollywood celebrities, and built the first luxury hotel there, the Flamingo, in 1946.

nation of criminal activities. The word "Mafia" has evolved to refer to the syndicate, or sometimes more specifically, to the syndicate's ruling elite. The boss, or "don," who headed each "family" exercised absolute power over all its members, who adhered to a strict code of silence, or "omerta," with regard to the society's inner workings. Maranzano became "boss of all bosses." Five months after he gave himself this title, Maranzano was murdered in his Manhattan office. Because of the Mafia's code of silence, there was never any proof as to the identity of his killer, but it is generally agreed that Maranzano's death was ordered by his rival, Charles "Lucky" Luciano.

When Maranzano was buried, so was the title "boss of all bosses." Heads of the "families" reorganized themselves into a seven-member national board, which most notably included Luciano, Meyer Lansky, Joe Adonis, and Frank Costello. This board gave orders to the syndicate and also mediated its internal disputes.

The emerging national crime syndicate incorporated not only Mafia families but also a conglomeration of other gangs that had blossomed during the Prohibition era. After the repeal of Prohibition (1933), the new syndicate divided up their already diversified interests in gambling, loan-sharking, prostitution, narcotics, labor racketeering, and protection among the various gangs. In order to make sure that the orders of the national board were carried out, its members decided to create an enforcement arm. So the 1930s saw the development of a cadre of professional killers, dubbed by the press as "Murder, Inc.," which carried out slayings on assignment. This outfit developed a slang that soon passed into the general American vocabulary—an assignment to kill, for example, was a "contract," and a target of assassination was a "hit." Albert Anastasia and Louis "Lepke" Buchalter, the biggest labor racketeer in the country, led this group of killers.

Police records show that Lepke began his career in crime in his early teens, picking pockets and stealing from local stores. By the mid-1920s, he had risen in the ranks of the underworld. When labor leaders sent over a request for a band of thugs to beat up local union rebels, Lepke's men did the work. But the beatings did not end after the fee was paid. Lepke proceeded to install his men in the union and saw to it that they were placed in positions of power. They voted to increase members' dues—and those who protested were beaten. The increase went into Lepke's pocket. The labor leaders were helpless since they themselves had brought the mob into the picture. Lepke used the same tactics on manufacturers who wanted strikers injured for causing trouble. Many owners soon found themselves working for organized crime. Those who refused to cooperate were beaten, their merchandise destroyed, or their place of business bombed. Formerly honest businessmen, especially in the fur, garment, and trucking industries, lived with fear and violence until they agreed to Lepke's terms.

Lepke followed the simple rule that if there were no witnesses to a crime, there could not be any indictment or trial. He sent witnesses out of the state under threat of death if they ever returned. When they disobeyed his orders, his killers hunted them down.

One of those who violated Lepke's orders was Max Rubin, a man who knew too much. Along with strict orders not to return to New York, Lepke had given Rubin money to go to the Catskills and then to New Orleans. Rubin got homesick, however, and slipped back into the city. In 1936, Lepke ordered Rubin killed. The gunmen left him for dead but Rubin survived. It was one of the worst mistakes Lepke ever made be-

"Dutch" Schultz on the eve of his 1935 trial for tax evasion. Schultz was tried twice on this charge, but the government failed to convict him. Hit men from Murder, Inc., gunned him down in a gang war in 1935.

cause Rubin's testimony would eventually send Lepke to the electric chair.

At last, law enforcement officers began to close in on Lepke. He was indicted for violation of the Anti-trust Act because of his control over the fur industry; and when the case came to trial in 1937, Lepke fled, ordering death for the witnesses who could be used against him. The underworld had never seen such a wave of murders as that which followed. Even Lepke's old pals were not certain who would be next.

For almost two years, Lepke hid while the manhunt continued. His name appeared on the FBI's most wanted list. New York's District Attorney Thomas E. Dewey offered a $25,000 reward—dead or alive—in a drive to break the gangster's hold on the city. Slowly, the underworld, which had hidden Lepke, turned against him, and before long there was a "contract" out on Lepke.

Columnist Walter Winchell, a friend of Hoover's, arranged a meeting between Lepke and Hoover in 1939. At the end of the meeting, Lepke turned himself in and was arrested. Soon after this, police arrested a minor mob member, Abe "Kid Twist" Reles, whose confessions implicated many important organized crime figures and, specifically, members of Murder, Inc. In the course of the ensuing investigations, Lepke was indicted for murder, convicted, and executed (1944) in the electric chair at Sing Sing prison. He was the only top-level syndicate leader ever to get the death penalty.

Just before he was to testify against Albert Anastasia and Benjamin "Bugsy" Siegel, another high-level gangster and notorious murderer, Reles died in a fall from a Brooklyn hotel window. It was never determined whether his death was accident, suicide, or murder. With Reles dead, the case against Anastasia and Siegel was weakened, and they were saved from going to court. Still, they were not safe from the mob, which, to protect its own interests, killed Siegel in 1947 and gunned down Anastasia ten years later in a barber shop on Seventh Avenue in New York City.

Murder, Inc. sometimes operated internally, acting against errant mobsters. A case in point was the mob-ordered shooting of Arthur Flegenheimer, known as Dutch Schultz, a founding member of the national crime syndicate, and one of the first to recognize the potential of the lucrative "numbers" racket. Bloodthirsty and unstable, Schultz had ordered the murders of the two rival bootleggers, Jack "Legs" Diamond and, a killer even more vicious and twisted than Schultz, Vincent "Mad Dog" Coll. But when the Dutchman asked the board of the national crime syndicate to approve the assassination of New York Special Prosecutor Thomas E. Dewey, the board refused, leery of becoming embroiled in political murders. Schultz vowed to get Dewey himself. Murder, Inc., struck first, however, gunning down Schultz in a Newark, New Jersey restaurant in 1935.

The syndicate reinvested the money it earned from bootlegging in other ventures, both criminal and "legitimate," and was eventually able to establish strong business and political interests in the U.S. It was able to gain such firm ground partly because Hoover long denied the existence of a national crime organization. As late as the 1950s he discouraged President Dwight D. Eisenhower's administration from probing into alleged syndicate operations, stating that, "No single individual or coalition of racketeers dominates organized crime across the nation."

But in 1957 police found dozens of gangland figures from major cities across the country meeting at a home in Apalachin, New York, to discuss the power play in the organization that led to Anastasia's death. Sixty members of the mob were arrested by local police, and Hoover could no longer ignore its existence. As a result of the Apalachin arrests, Attorney General William P. Rogers established the Special Group on Organized Crime. This group, in operation for two years, had some success in prosecuting syndicate members. Hoover, however, impeded the Special Group's investigations by refusing to allow access to FBI files containing important information on organized crime.

Hoover's reluctance to investigate organized crime may have stemmed from a fear for his own life, or maybe he sincerely doubted the existence of the mob as an investigatable

Jack "Legs" Diamond (second from left) with his attorneys. Diamond, a racketeer and bootlegger, had many enemies. There were four attempts on his life before two Murder, Inc., assassins finally killed him on December 18, 1931.

Marlon Brando as Don Corleone discusses "family" business with Robert Duvall in the 1972 film *The Godfather*. Based on the novel by Mario Puzo, the movie portrayed the traditions, personalities, and inner workings of organized crime.

and ultimately prosecutable organization. Nevertheless, he did launch the "Top Hoodlum" program in November 1957. FBI officers in cities throughout the United States listed names of mobsters whom they considered the ten most dangerous. These men became priority targets for FBI investigations. This program still exists.

Over the years the FBI has used various techniques in its attempts to gain evidence against organized crime figures. One of these is wiretapping, first used by the FBI in Chicago in 1959 when agents concluded that a restaurant was serving as a headquarters for some "top hoodlums." With Hoover's approval, the agents planted microphones in the restaurant so to be able to hear the gangsters' conversation. Attorney General Robert F. Kennedy also encouraged the use of microphones and wiretaps in his fight against organized crime during the early 1960s.

In 1970, congress passed the Organized Crime Control Act. This legislation expanded the FBI's jurisdiction, enabling the agency to investigate gambling and other rackets in which the syndicate might be involved; instituted a witness protection program, whereby informants could be granted immunity from prosecution in exchange for their cooperation; and also secured the legality of the use of electronic surveillance, at the time an issue of controversy. Further legislation, the Racketeer-Influenced and Corrupt Organizations Act, allowed the law to prosecute for mob-related activity, rather than only for specific crimes. This legislation made mob leaders, who always had others do the actual dirty work, more vulnerable to investigation and prosecution.

The FBI of the 1980s, led by FBI Director William H. Webster, continues to find the 1970s legislation invaluable in the battle against organized crime. With the help of Ronald Goldstock, the director of the New York State Task Force on Organized Crime, and Rudolph W. Giuliani, U.S. attorney for the Southern District of New York, indictments were served against nine significant Mafia figures in 1985, including leaders of the five major New York families. There have been an increasing number of high-ranking organized crime figures willing to testify in court in exchange for immunity and protection, and as a result convictions have become more numerous. Also, infighting, always indicative of organizational instability, has emerged as individuals seek to fill the gaps left vacant by convicted leaders and families hasten to protect themselves from the testimonies of informants. The December 1985 shooting of organized crime leader Paul Castellano shortly before he was to testify in a trial involving key mob figures is recent evidence of this current infighting, and attests to the fact that the FBI is beating organized crime from the inside out. As a result of combined FBI and local police efforts there were some 60 organized-crime-related trials in process throughout the country in the mid-eighties.

Vito Genovese, narcotics kingpin for whom gang leaders revived the title "boss of all bosses" in 1957. Genovese's bungled attempt to murder underling Joseph Valachi induced Valachi to testify at the 1963 Senate hearings on organized crime.

A little boy gives the Nazi salute at the opening of the German-American Bund camp in New Jersey about 1935. The Bund, which held the same beliefs as did the Nazi party in Germany, was under continuous FBI surveillance.

6

Spies and Saboteurs

The FBI began its war against foreign spies long before the Japanese attack on Pearl Harbor thrust the United States into World War II. In the fall of 1939, shortly after the German invasion of Poland, President Franklin D. Roosevelt authorized the FBI to coordinate all investigative matters involving espionage, sabotage, subversive activities, and internal security. The war years saw an increased number of spy rings operating in the United States. The sabotage and espionage controls of the FBI proved to be a major contribution in the nation's successful struggle to defeat the Axis nations.

Before the United States entered the war, German agents had organized a pro-Nazi group, called the German-American Bund, which had chapters in many large American cities. The FBI kept a sharp watch on the Bund's activities, membership, teachings, and its military-style training program. FBI infiltrators joined the group and were accepted as committed Nazis, learning the secrets of the Bund. Although the Bund promoted itself as a group concerned about friendship between the United States and Germany, reports from within the organization convinced the FBI otherwise. The real aim of the Bund was to disrupt American industries in the event of war.

Important information came to light because of the Bureau's infiltration of the Bund. There was a fantastic Nazi plot, for example, to steal secret plans for the defense of the East coast of the United States by luring a high-ranking army officer to a New York hotel room, overpowering him, and seizing the plans. The FBI thwarted another plot in February 1938 when a Bund member tried to steal 35 blank American passports by impersonating a State Department official. That spy was Guenther Rumrich and his arrest followed immediately.

Rumrich was among the first of the enemy spies to be arrested. It soon became apparent, however, that a more organized system of counterespionage was essential. Little could be accomplished by arresting spies after their damaging work had been done. In order to prevent sabotage, it would be necessary to know the innermost workings of enemy espionage—the extent of their networks, their plans for causing damage, and their interest in highly secret military information. The FBI, realizing that Germany already had many skillfully trained agents, expected a wave of sabotage. The Bureau drew up comprehensive plans, outlining its anticipated functions. The FBI now had its most important job—protecting the internal security of the United States.

The burden of training new and veteran FBI agents in the techniques and methods of counterespionage fell upon the instructors of the FBI Academy. Congress appropriated the funds for an FBI barracks for special training at the Marine Corps base at Quantico, Virginia. At the peak of its wartime expansion program, 1,000 men were in training at the same time.

Reports to the FBI regarding suspicious activities reached flood proportions as the Germans won victory after victory in Europe. In 1939, as many as 1,650 matters involving internal security required investigation. The number of reports by concerned citizens rapidly increased. On one day in May 1940, more than 2,800 complaints reached FBI headquarters.

New field offices opened in Hawaii, Puerto Rico, and Alaska. A new security division was created at FBI headquarters in Washington to coordinate national investigations involving sabotage, espionage, sedition, and other war-related matters. Its responsibility—to spy on the spy.

The entire Western Hemisphere stood in great danger of a foreign invasion during the war years of 1941 and 1942. Reports reached the FBI that German troops waited at Dakar, West Africa, for the right moment to strike at Brazil. Further reports revealed that Nazi dictator Adolf Hitler planned a direct attack on American defenses in the Caribbean. German and Japanese planes were expected to attack the Panama Canal. A fleet of submarines reportedly stood ready to carry Nazi troops into Colombia and Venezuela. Captured plans re-

Spectators line the streets to watch a German-American Bund parade in New York City in 1937. The organization of Nazi sympathizers dissolved in 1939.

vealed that a ship would be sunk in a narrow channel in Dutch Guiana (now called Suriname), cutting off 60% of a mineral essential for U.S. industries. Reports from Brazil indicated that Japanese nationals in that country were arming.

In spite of all these reports, the countries of the Americas remained unprepared. The shock of the December 7, 1941, attack on the U.S. naval base at Pearl Harbor, Hawaii, suddenly made South American countries alert to the prospects of a similar attack. For more than two years, the FBI had found enemy spying in the United States closely linked with Nazi activities in South America. When informed of this, many of these nations requested FBI liaison agents to work with their

FBI employees view Japanese contraband seized in searches of alien Japanese property in the United States. By order of President Franklin D. Roosevelt (1882–1945), approximately 110,000 Japanese-Americans were taken from their homes and moved to relocation camps in 1942 as a security measure. Hoover opposed the relocation.

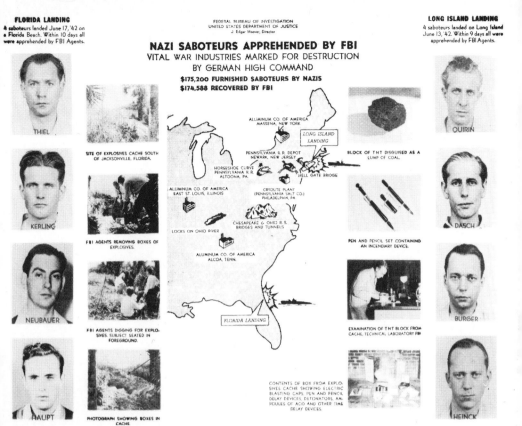

FLORIDA LANDING

4 saboteurs landed June 17, '42 on a Florida Beach. Within 10 days all were apprehended by FBI Agents.

FEDERAL BUREAU OF INVESTIGATION
UNITED STATES DEPARTMENT OF JUSTICE
J. Edgar Hoover, Director

LONG ISLAND LANDING

4 saboteurs landed on Long Island June 13, '42. Within 9 days all were apprehended by FBI Agents.

NAZI SABOTEURS APPREHENDED BY FBI
VITAL WAR INDUSTRIES MARKED FOR DESTRUCTION BY GERMAN HIGH COMMAND
$175,200 FURNISHED SABOTEURS BY NAZIS
$174,588 RECOVERED BY FBI

In 1938 President Roosevelt authorized the FBI to conduct investigations into potential German sabotage and espionage. This chart shows some of the Nazi saboteurs arrested by the Bureau, and a map of the saboteurs' intended targets.

own intelligence forces. Others sent men to train at FBI schools. In this way, an effective pan-American intelligence force was successfully created to oppose and destroy Nazi spy and sabotage rings throughout the Americas.

Altogether, from July 1, 1940, through June 30, 1946, South American nations either expelled, interned, or removed far inland more than 15,000 Axis spies and sympathizers. Over 450 suspected saboteurs were apprehended. Thirty secret short-wave radio stations used to transmit information about the United States to Germany were put out of operation.

The most daring and spectacular Nazi espionage act in the United States occurred on June 12, 1942. A German submarine landed four saboteurs near Amagansett, Long Island. At the same time, another submarine landed a second group of Nazi saboteurs near Jacksonville, Florida. Their orders were to destroy key American war plants, bridges, and railroad stations. Their list included the plants of the Aluminum Corporation of America in Tennessee, New York, and Illinois; New York City's Hell Gate bridge; the locks on the Ohio River between Pittsburgh and Louisville; and the Horseshoe Curve of the Pennsylvania Railroad in Altoona, Pennsylvania.

Hitler believed that a small detachment of highly trained saboteurs could greatly slow down America's military capacity thereby enabling the Nazis to consolidate their European military gains. The saboteurs had been carefully trained and equipped. They had learned how to use explosives and incendiary bombs. They had studied ways of damaging industrial machinery. They had pored over maps of the United States in order to know the exact location of the targets. Their English was flawless. They carried forged Social Security cards, birth certificates, and driver's licenses, and their mission had the personal approval of Nazi Germany's highest leaders.

Starting with the initial landing, their mission came apart. An alert member of the Coast Guard on the Amagansett beach spotted the landing and informed the FBI. Hoover ordered the Bureau into action. Within two weeks, all the saboteurs had been arrested. This carefully planned, grandiose scheme of the Nazis ended quickly. The FBI had thwarted a major threat to America's internal security.

The Nazis tried again. In November 1944 a German submarine put ashore saboteurs near Crab Tree Point, Maine. This time a teenager, the son of a local deputy sheriff, became suspicious when he noticed men walking along the beach without winter coats. He, too, notified the FBI. Within one month the Bureau had captured these enemy agents, before they could carry out their mission.

Throughout the war years, the FBI investigated almost 20,000 cases of suspected sabotage. Watchful and cooperative workmen in industrial plants reported all suspicious events to the FBI. Most of these reports proved to be from alert but overexcited citizens. Yet, the complaints had to be investigated. All in all, not one case of enemy-directed sabotage was successful. Neither the Germans nor the Japanese were able to establish an apparatus capable of crippling or destroying America's wartime effort.

The war created an extraordinary need for industrial security. The FBI, at the request of the Army and Navy, surveyed more than 2,200 factories and suggested ways of tightening security. In addition, the Bureau trained local law enforcement agents in handling civil defense, convoy traffic, protection of public utilities, and the investigation of espionage and subversion. More than 73,000 of these agents attended FBI training programs between 1940 and 1943.

J. Edgar Hoover and the FBI guarded the home front, and they guarded it extremely well. Whatever boasts Hoover made about the efficiency of the Bureau were shown to be entirely justified during this turbulent period.

FBI special agents go through firing drills at the FBI rifle range in Quantico, Virginia. Agents receive extensive firearms training, and many become expert marksmen.

Senator Joseph R. McCarthy (1908–1957) and his chief coun-
sel, Roy Cohn, confer behind a box containing files on alleged
communists during the Army-McCarthy hearings in 1954.
McCarthy launched his anticommunist crusade with a 1950
announcement that he had a list, based on FBI findings, of
205 U.S. State Department employees who were card-carry-
ing Communist party members.

7

Dissent and Unrest

After World War II, Communist nations increased their subversive activities in the United States. The Soviet Union wanted, above all, information about the atomic bomb. Once again, the Bureau started intelligence operations, this time investigating espionage rings during what was ostensibly peacetime, but was often called the Cold War. Anticommunism became the theme of FBI investigations throughout the 1950s, 1960s, and 1970s. To Hoover and the FBI, Communists, real or imagined, were present in every aspect of American life—and had to be watched.

During the Cold War years of the late 1940s and the 1950s, the COMINFIL (Communist infiltration) program of the FBI led to the investigation of thousands of people. The mere accusation, by any caliber of informant, that someone was a Communist or involved with supposedly Communist-affiliated groups could ruin his career and reputation.

In fact, the whole period was strongly reminiscent of the "Red Scare" under Palmer in the 1920s. Many politicians capitalized on the American people's fear of Communism, none more sensationally than Senator Joseph R. McCarthy of Wisconsin. Hoover was a close friend of McCarthy, with whom he shared a deep concern about the perceived threat of Communist infiltration of U.S. society. The FBI worked closely with the investigations of those suspected of being Communists or belonging to left-wing organizations.

One of the most famous and controversial cases of the day was the trial of Alger Hiss, a highly regarded, former State Department official accused of membership in a Communist espionage ring. The FBI was deeply involved in the case against Hiss from beginning to end. Since 1939 the FBI had kept a file on Hiss because a former Communist, Whittaker Chambers, accused him of being a fellow party member. The FBI watched Hiss for years, without his knowledge, but found no evidence to support Chambers's claim. Then, with McCarthy's rise to power, Congress began to take seriously his allegations that the State Department was riddled with Communists. Chambers testified in 1948 before the House Un-American Activities Committee that in the 1930s Hiss had belonged to the same spy ring as Chambers and had given Chambers classified State Department documents. Hiss denied all charges of spying or of having used Chambers as a courier. On the basis of the papers that Chambers supplied, Hiss was convicted of perjury and spent three years in prison.

The FBI claimed a great victory. But many regarded the evidence against Hiss as highly suspect, and there were even charges that it had been fabricated. Hiss himself always maintained his innocence and in the 1980s was still struggling to get his conviction overturned. In 1975 the attorney general ordered, under the Freedom of Information Act, the release of the FBI files on Hiss. Most of these documents have since been made public, but they have not been conclusive either way.

In the 1960s, dissent in America reached epidemic proportions. A kaleidoscope of issues ignited the protesters. This was the civil rights era, as blacks and many whites sought to end the inequities created by centuries of segregation and discrimination. It was also the age of the Vietnam War, an unpopular war that provoked widespread demonstrations.

Students across America marched, rallied, and protested on college campuses, thrusting their causes and demands into the national spotlight. At Columbia, Harvard, Berkeley, the University of California at Los Angeles, and other academic institutions, the scene was the same: demonstration after demonstration attracted thousands of chanting rebellious students, all focused on the cause at hand. Burning of draft cards, the American flag, and other symbols of the social order became a common sight at rallies as students replaced the establishment's symbols with their own, the peace sign and the black power fist. Although students were not the only group to protest, the issues of civil rights for minorities, protection of the environment, and women's equality found their strongest supporters in colleges and universities.

Campus activism, especially in regard to the Vietnam War, spread to many of America's colleges. The sit-ins, peaceful at first, grew larger, more frequent, and gradually more violent as students took over administration buildings, damaged university property, and occasionally shut down schools com-

Left to right: California congressman Richard Nixon, Chief Investigator Robert Stripling, and Chairman J. Parnell Thomas of the House Un-American Activities Committee (HUAC). This committee, given permanent status in 1945, was formed in 1938 under Representative Martin Dies, who claimed that communists had infiltrated the government.

Lauren Bacall and Humphrey Bogart head a delegation of movie celebrities visiting Washington, D.C., in 1947 to protest HUAC investigations into alleged Hollywood communism. As Senator McCarthy's campaign gained momentum, the Hollywood blacklist ruined the careers of many innocent people in the film industry.

pletely. When administrators called in police forces to end the challenge to authority, arrests, injuries, and occasionally even the death of some students resulted.

Hoover regarded virtually all protest against American policies, political or social, as Communist-inspired. In a 1963 discussion about Communist influence in America, he stated: "They have infiltrated every conceivable sphere of activity; youth groups; radio; television; the motion picture industry; minority groups; and civil and political units."

In the 1960s, the FBI developed the COINTEL (counterintelligence) program, which investigated alleged subversive groups, their members, and their activities, both personal and professional. Between 1960 and 1974, the FBI conducted more than 500,000 domestic intelligence investigations. FBI field offices summarized on a semimonthly basis the programs and activities of all civil rights and black nationalist organizations, reported on the speeches, writings, and activities of the "New Left," and maintained surveillance on anti-Vietnam War demonstrations and student organizations on college campuses. The women's liberation movement was also investigated. The FBI even spied on such moderate civil rights organizations as the National Association for the Advancement of Colored People.

Congressional investigations have shown that the FBI often used illegal techniques in its efforts to maintain internal security. For example, when the internationally renowned civil

Former State Department official Alger Hiss before the House Un-American Activities Committee, August 3, 1948. Charged with being active in a Soviet espionage ring, Hiss was later convicted of perjury when he claimed not to have had contact during a certain period with Whittaker Chambers, one of the ring's couriers.

rights leader, the Reverend Martin Luther King, Jr., criticized the FBI for its lack of zeal in protecting the civil rights of American blacks, Hoover called Dr. King "the most notorious liar in the country." He then invited reporters to hear tapes of Dr. King's personal conversations as evidence that "moral degenerates," as Hoover phrased it, were leading the civil rights movement. His hatred of Martin Luther King caused the director to place at least two dozen illegal wiretaps on King's telephones and electronic "bugs" in his hotel rooms. He ordered that a tape of a party where King was allegedly compromised be mailed to the civil rights leader's wife. Hoover also sent an unsigned letter to King strongly suggesting that he commit suicide.

King was not the only public leader whose personal life was under FBI scrutiny. Hoover regaled many attorneys general and presidents with racy stories about the lives of famous people. It was claimed that Hoover kept a personal file on every politician who passed through Washington. Perhaps because of the nature of the FBI's work, or perhaps because of Hoover's prestige, or perhaps out of fear of blackmail, every successive president reappointed him. After his death, however, Congress limited the tenure of FBI directors to one ten-year term.

Only after Hoover had died did the country begin to learn the full extent of some of his abuses of power. A month after Hoover's death, the Watergate break-in triggered congressional and journalistic investigations that revealed, among other abuses of federal power, widespread wrongdoings by the FBI. These investigations of the FBI soon produced a series of spectacular revelations about the inside operations of the Bureau under Hoover. The Senate Select Committee on Intelligence disclosed that Hoover had done political investigations for presidents Franklin D. Roosevelt, John F. Kennedy, Lyndon B. Johnson, and Richard M. Nixon. Johnson, for example, had sought personal information about Senator Barry Goldwater, his 1964 presidential opponent.

Hoover also kept files on the sexual activities of many public officials. Most revealing, however, was information about the tactics used by Hoover's counterintelligence program, COINTELPRO, begun in 1956. These methods included attempts to create internal dissension within certain groups by mailing anonymous letters, efforts to get some workers fired by informing employers of the workers' political views, illegal wiretappings, and burglaries. The Bureau had, for example, stirred up internal dissent within several black nationalist groups that led to killings among the members. A Senate committee called these COINTELPRO activities "indisputably degrading to a free society."

The Senate committee also criticized the FBI's investigation of President Kennedy's assassination, claiming that it focused too narrowly on the alleged killer, Lee Harvey Oswald, and thus failed to follow other leads.

President Nixon appointed L. Patrick Gray as Hoover's successor. Gray introduced some needed reforms, including the hiring of women as special agents. He resigned in 1973 and was replaced by Clarence Kelley, the police chief of Kansas City, Missouri.

Director Kelley did much to correct these types of abuses, and he tried to put the FBI firmly back under the Department of Justice's control. With the election of President Carter, Kelley was replaced as director by William H. Webster.

The controversy surrounding FBI activities under Hoover will probably never be resolved. There are those who claim that Hoover and the FBI recognized a legitimate threat to U.S.

security and the means they used were necessary to protect the nation. Others disagree. To them, the FBI continually misunderstood democratic dissent and misread the goals of those who sought change through legitimate procedures guaranteed in the Bill of Rights.

The FBI has also investigated members of Congress. The prime example of this was the Abscam operation—the name is derived from *Arab* and *scam*, or swindle—after which 19

Mrs. Annie Lee Moss, a civilian army employee, breaks down in a Capitol corridor after being accused (1954) by Senator McCarthy of Communist party membership. Her son comforts her. The FBI often conducted extensive investigations of individuals based solely on McCarthy's allegations of subversion.

Julius and Ethel Rosenberg, after apprehension by the FBI, were executed in 1953 for conveying information about the atomic bomb to the Soviet Union. The case is still controversial—some feel the Rosenbergs were framed, others believe that they were guilty of treason.

Charismatic black leader Malcolm X at a Black Muslim rally in New York City. FBI attempts to infiltrate the Black Muslims, a militant separatist group, were hampered in the 1960s because the Bureau had so few minority members.

persons, 7 of them U.S. congressmen, were convicted of bribery or conspiracy in 1980 and 1981.

Abscam was a controversial program in which FBI agents, disguised as representatives of an Arab sheik, offered money to politically influential individuals in return for legislative favors. For example, Michael Myers, a representative from Pennsylvania, accepted $15,000 in return for a promise to help the fictional sheik gain political asylum, or government protection. Secret cameras and tape recorders used during the negotiations between the disguised agents and the political figures gave the FBI definite proof that the men had accepted the bribes.

Civil rights leader Martin Luther King, Jr. (1929–1968; first row, seventh from right) leads a 1965 march on Washington, D.C. Hoover viewed King as "immoral" and used the FBI to carry out a vendetta against him.

In one of the largest mass protests in history, an estimated half-million peaceful marchers converged on Washington, D.C., for Moratorium Day (November 15, 1969), demanding withdrawal of U.S. troops from Vietnam. These protests became a major concern of the FBI, which monitored the anti-war movement.

All seven congressmen attempted to appeal their convictions to the United States Supreme Court, but the Court denied their requests, stating that the defendants were all "willing volunteers" in corrupt activity. The Abscam operation was generally praised as being a gallant effort against political corruption, but some believed that the undercover agents tempted the public officials to engage in a crime they might not have otherwise committed, a procedure known as entrapment. Nevertheless, it was a significant investigation in American history because it raised the issue of how the nation could effectively police its own lawmakers.

Dr. Martin Luther King, Jr., gazes through the bars of his cell in the Jefferson County Courthouse in Birmingham, Alabama, in 1967. King, for years under FBI surveillance, criticized the Bureau for its lack of zeal in protecting the civil rights of American blacks.

8

Freedom of Information Act

Everybody compiles a written record of his or her life. Birth certificates, academic transcripts, school yearbooks, driver's licenses, credit card applications, loan payments, employment evaluations, medical records, hospital charts, dental X-rays, and even death certificates contain information about how we live, look, spend our money, and die. These records show where we were born, the schools we attended and the grades received, where we purchased items, and what we paid. School yearbooks list clubs we joined and athletic events in which we participated. Driver's licences contain our height, weight, and in many cases a photograph. Often petitions signed, especially those addressed to the president of the United States, are preserved in the National Archives. Government agencies also have information about us (social security records, taxes, etc.). It has been only since the passage of the Freedom of Information Act (FOIA) in 1966 that an individual can obtain any file that the government may have concerning one's activities.

The storage capabilities of today's computers enable the government to keep voluminous files on individuals and groups. Because data from these files can be made available to strangers for unknown purposes, it is important for individuals to have knowledge of and access to any personal information about them kept by government agencies. By enacting the FOIA in 1966 (it was amended and strengthened in 1974), Congress gave individuals the right to know what their government files contain and the means to change this information if it can be proved erroneous. Since 1966, most government agencies have cooperated with requests for personal information. The files of the FBI, however, have proven more difficult to obtain, because the Bureau believes that disclosure of such information could compromise agents and their sources. Nevertheless, it is possible for an individual to obtain copies of their FBI files.

In order to do its job effectively, the FBI must work secretly. Most of its files are not public. Secrecy is essential to protect the Bureau's agents and their sources as well as methods of operations. (Not until 1985 did the FBI release most, but not all, of its file on John Dillinger.)

Long before the FOIA was enacted, the FBI had become an intelligence-gathering body answerable to no one but its director. The full extent of FBI activities is still not known. It is known, however, that the FBI unlawfully harassed and kept files on political dissidents, maintained illegal surveillance of civil rights and political activists organizations, and waged vendettas against leading political figures for no other reason than that the Bureau did not like their beliefs or their politics. For years, the FBI maintained an exhaustive surveillance of Martin Luther King, Jr., Malcolm X, and many other leaders, both black and white, who were active in the civil rights movement of the 1960s. (When the Martin Luther King file was released in the early 1980s under the FOIA, its 44,873 pages had been so heavily edited that the substantive content was virtually eliminated. Nevertheless, a careful study of the material shows that J. Edgar Hoover considered King a Marxist "tool" of the Soviet Union.)

President Dwight D. Eisenhower (1890–1969) bestows the National Security Medal on J. Edgar Hoover at a 1955 White House ceremony. Relations between Hoover and Eisenhower were cordial.

Under Presidents Gerald R. Ford and Jimmy Carter, reform of the FBI and strengthening the means by which private citizens could obtain official information greatly corrected these abuses of power. The check on an overzealous FBI is now provided by Congress, which has appointed special committees on intelligence matters to oversee Bureau activities.

Government maintenance of files on its citizens is not a recent phenomenon. In the late 19th century, for example, labor and agrarian protesters suffered from blacklisting as police, both private and government, kept dossiers on those considered dangerous. During the "Red Scare" of 1919–20, files were kept on thousands of purportedly disloyal Americans, many of whom were illegally detained. These files, now available in the National Archives, show that unsubstantiated charges of subversion and disloyalty from a multitude of untrained informants were accepted as fact and used to harass and imprison innocent Americans.

The FBI files also reveal that during the years of Prohibition, 1920–33, scores of Americans were wrongfully accused of criminal offenses through the use of hearsay and questionable information. Many states kept similar files. In New York, for example, state police records were used by a legislative investigating committee in 1920 to remove hundreds of people from their jobs and to accuse others falsely of un-American activities.

The advent of computers expanded the government's data base on allegedly suspicious individuals. J. Edgar Hoover's first General Intelligence Division index in 1920 contained about 450,000 names. Currently, there are more than 20 million names in the FBI files.

Modern technological innovations in communications have widened intelligence-gathering capabilities. Wiretaps and electronic "bugs" have become the uninvited witnesses to thousands of private conversations, covertly intruding upon the fundamental right of privacy.

Few would deny that the government has the obligation to insure public safety and to safeguard national security. But this obligation must be weighed against the rights guaranteed to citizens by the Bill of Rights. Fortunately, an alert Congress has tightened its supervision of the FBI, and the passage of the FOIA has given citizens the opportunity to know what is in their FBI files as well as the right to correct erroneous data.

The FOIA requires all agencies of the executive branch of government to reply promptly to requests for personal files, and it sets specified time limits within which the agency must respond. The law stipulates that the fee charged for copying and searching for records must be reasonable, and that any agency may reduce or waive fees if the information released benefits the public. Agencies are permitted to withhold records on several grounds, such as protection of the privacy of another individual, maintaining confidentiality of sources, and guarding against the impairment of national security or the foreign relations of the United States. There is no need to give a reason for requesting government records. Within the exemptions cited, one has an absolute right to know what information is in government files. No other government in the world has such a law.

Under the Privacy Act (1974), an individual can correct and even destroy governmental records (with the exception of those kept by the CIA) if these records are false. The Privacy Act also sets restrictions on what kind of information about an individual a governmental agency may collect and disseminate. Information acquired about American citizens must be both *relevant* and *necessary* to the agency in carrying out a specific authorized purpose. The FBI, for example, is now prohibited from recording personal information about an individual or his or her activities if that person is not connected with an official FBI investigation.

Since the FOIA and the Privacy Act were enacted, the FBI has received more than 100,000 requests from private citizens, organizations, scholars, and newspaper reporters. The FOIA may help to deter against future violations of the Bill of Rights.

A 1973 Gallup Poll showed that 85 percent of the population (including 85 percent of those under thirty) had a "highly favorable" or "favorable" opinion of the FBI. This figure dropped slightly to 80 percent in 1975. The 1975 survey showed that college students were more critical of the FBI than the rest of the public. An earlier Gallup survey conducted in 1965 showed that 77 percent of parents would be pleased if their child became an FBI agent. While we do not have current survey figures, the overall evaluation of the FBI is probably still quite favorable.

Should I ask the FBI if they have a file on me? Why not? The goal of the FOIA is to give every person the right to hold governmental agencies accountable and to keep them within the Constitution. Conservative columnist Garry Wills wrote: "Sending for one's file is a patriotic duty." All citizens should consider sending for their file. Even the Government Printing Office publishes *A Citizen's Guide on How to Use the Freedom of Information Act and the Privacy Act in Requesting Governmental Documents.*

The following is a sample letter for requesting records:

Your name
Address
Date
Social Security Number
Date of Birth

Freedom of Information/Privacy Act Unit
Federal Bureau of Investigation
Washington, D.C. 20535

Gentlemen:

    This is a request under the FOIA. I request a complete search for all records maintained by your agency pertaining to (me) (name of organization) (or description of subject matter).

    If any documents are denied in whole or in part, please explain why and which exemption is claimed by your agency. Please explain if any records pertaining to my request have been destroyed.

    If the fee is in excess of $_____, consult me before proceeding.

Yours sincerely,

(Notarized signature plus your title if you are writing on behalf of an organization)

The FOIA requires an agency to respond to your request within ten business days after receiving it. The FBI, because of the large number of requests, simply sends an acknowledgment stating that processing is in order of receipt. It may be necessary for the FBI to request additional information to help distinguish you from others with the same or similar name. This is usually true where information is in a file which does not have your name in its title.

While the FOIA does provide for the right of appeal if

records are denied, it would be most unusual to file such an appeal as the FBI will eventually respond to your request. After 30 days, it is possible to telephone the FBI Freedom of Information Act Unit at (202)-324-5520, and, after identifying yourself, they should be able to tell you when the documents requested will be sent to you. While material involving ongoing investigations and material considered national security matters cannot be released, more than 90 percent of requests received by the FBI are processed fairly and expeditiously. If after following these simple procedures, you still encounter problems, refer the matter to your congressman.

The FOIA is a tribute to American democracy and to the belief that the people have a right to know what government files contain. Rather than a government removed from the people, the FOIA demonstrates that our nation is truly of the people, by the people, and for the people.

In 1961 Hoover meets with President John F. Kennedy (1917–1963) and his brother Robert (1925–1968), then attorney general. Hoover and the younger Kennedy were on the same side during the McCarthy era, but the Kennedys later clashed with him on civil rights issues and over the ultimate control of the Bureau.

FBI Director J. Edgar Hoover at his desk in 1954. He was
appointed by Attorney General Harlan Fiske Stone in 1924.

9

Becoming an FBI Agent

Writing in 1954, J. Edgar Hoover stated that "There are some things required of Special Agents of the FBI which cannot be taught; they are the qualities that are embodied in our motto—Fidelity, Bravery, Integrity." In that year, 6,000 men wore the FBI badge. Today, more than 8,000 men and women are special agents. And every year the FBI hires additional young people and trains them in investigative procedures. They are assigned to the FBI's field offices located throughout the United States. Virtually every racial, ethnic, and religious group in America is represented in the FBI.

Today, the Bureau is responsible not only for its original duties but hundreds of others, including detecting and apprehending espionage agents; investigating interstate automobile thefts; maintaining crime laboratories for its own use and to aid local and state law enforcement agencies; investigating kidnappings, some cases of arson, bank robberies, interstate transportation of stolen property, interstate gambling, and vi-

L. Patrick Gray III, appointed by President Richard M. Nixon to head the FBI after Hoover died. Although Gray introduced many needed reforms in the Bureau, he was forced to resign when it was learned he had destroyed sensitive documents concerning the Watergate break-in.

Cynthia Edgar, one of two women lawyers who sued Hoover in 1971 after he rejected their applications to become FBI agents. A year later, acting Director L. Patrick Gray overturned Hoover's long-standing refusal to hire women as special agents.

An agent examines fingerprint charts at FBI headquarters in Washington, D.C. in 1971. Keeping fingerprint records remains an important aspect of FBI operations.

olations of the 1964 Civil Rights Act; enforcing the 1965 Voting Rights Act; apprehending draft evaders; and investigating possible assassination attempts against the president or the vice president. The FBI also has dozens of intelligence and national security functions delegated to it by Congress.

The FBI's highly trained special agents are assigned to 59 field offices throughout the United States and to FBI headquarters in Washington, D.C. Each field office is under the charge of a special agent who reports to the director in Washington.

FBI employees are members of the federal civil service. Appointments and promotions are made on the basis of merit. Nearly every FBI executive or supervisor has risen through the staff ranks. In order to be eligible for the competitive written examination for becoming an FBI special agent, a candidate must:

1. Be a United States citizen
2. Be available for assignment anywhere within the Bureau's jurisdiction
3. Be between the ages of 23 and 35
4. Have excellent vision and hearing
5. Possess a valid driver's license
6. Be in excellent health

An applicant must also meet one of the following educational requirements:

1. Be a law school graduate
2. Be a college graduate with a major in accounting, economics, business, or finance
3. Be a college graduate and be fluent in foreign languages for which the Bureau has a need
4. Be a college graduate and have three years of full-time work experience
5. Hold a graduate degree and have two years of full-time work experience
6. Be a college graduate with a major in electrical engineering or metallurgy
7. Hold a graduate degree in physics, chemistry, biology, geology, pharmacy, pharmacology,

toxicology, mathematics, or engineering

8. Hold a graduate degree in business or public administration or computer science, or hold a graduate degree with a major emphasis on analysis and development of business/financial information systems

9. Have a college degree and three years of professional experience in biology, engineering, geology, pharmacy, or toxicology

10. Hold a college degree and have three years of experience as a systems or programming analyst handling business/financial systems

Applicants who meet these qualifications must take a written examination, which is graded by computer. Those who pass the written test are then formally interviewed by three trained FBI agents. Upon completion of both the written exam and the interview, applicants are numerically ranked with candidates from across the country.

Those who are selected are sent to the FBI's Training Academy in Quantico, Virginia, for 15 weeks. The training

An FBI special agent displays jewelry stolen from the Hotel Pierre in New York in 1972. The value of the jewels, recovered by the FBI in Detroit a week after the heist, was estimated at $750,000.

Clarence Kelley, appointed by President Richard Nixon in 1973, served as FBI director until 1978.

William Webster, the director of the FBI since 1978. A judge from St. Louis, Webster was appointed FBI director by President Carter when Clarence Kelley retired in 1978. Webster seeks to make the FBI a model of "professionalism" and constitutional awareness.

program covers more than 100 subjects dealing with law enforcement, including crime detection, fingerprinting, interviewing procedures, techniques for searching the scene of a crime, and federal criminal procedures. The proper use of firearms is taught and there is a strenuous physical education program. Agents who pass this 15-week course are indeed specialists in crime detection and law enforcement. They are able to analyze a minute particle of paint and help determine the year and make of the automobile from which it came, and to study a lipstick stain and be able to discover the trade name

91

and manufacturer of the lipstick. They are able to spot a forged document, and to tell whether a tiny strand of hair came from a human or from an animal. They acquire numerous other crime-detection skills as well. A career with the FBI can be a fascinating one for those interested in law enforcement.

The FBI's new headquarters, named after J. Edgar Hoover, was completed in 1975 at a cost of $126 million. Plans for the new building received congressional approval in 1962. Prior to its construction, the FBI occupied part of the Department of Justice building.

FURTHER READING

Buitrago, Ann and Immerman, Leon. *FBI Files.* New York: Grove Press, 1981.

Leuchtenburg, William. *The Perils of Prosperity: 1914–1932.* Chicago: University of Chicago Press, 1958.

Lowenthal, Max. *The Federal Bureau of Investigation.* Westport, Connecticut: Greenwood Press, 1950.

Powers, Richard. *G-Men.* Carbondale, Illinois: Southern Illinois University Press, 1983.

Whitehead, Don. *The FBI Story.* New York: Random House, 1956.

INDEX

94